Navy Spouse's

D0372473

Navy Spouse's Guide
Second Edition

Laura Hall Stavridis

Naval Institute Press
ANNAPOLIS, MARYLAND

Naval Institute Press
291 Wood Road
Annapolis, MD 21402

Library of Congress Cataloging-in-Publication Data
Stavridis, Laura Hall, 1959–
Navy spouse's guide / Laura Hall Stavridis—2nd ed.
  p. cm.
  Includes bibliographical references and index.
  ISBN 1-55750-870-4 (alk. paper)
  1. Navy spouses. 2. United States. Navy. I. Title.
V736 .S73 2002
359.1'0973—dc21   2001042565

Printed in the United States of America on acid-free paper ∞
09 08 07 06   9 8 7 6 5 4 3

"America Loves Its Citizens" reprinted with permission from the December 2000 *Proceedings,* © U.S. Naval Institute

"I Attended the *Cole* Memorial" reprinted with permission from the December 2000 *Proceedings,* © U.S. Naval Institute

"Deployments in the Electronic Age" reprinted with permission from Laurie Capen

To my navy family: my husband, Jim, and my two daughters, Christina and Julia. Thanks for your love and support during this project, and always.

Contents

Preface to the Second Edition

When I first sat down to write this book several years ago, I had three principal objectives in mind. First, I wanted to produce a simple user-friendly guide that would serve as both a basic introduction and a source of information about navy life for the many spouses who "join up" every year. Second, it seemed to me that neither a book nor another reference was available to talk in a direct, common-sense manner about various issues confronting spouses in the rapidly changing U.S. Navy of the twenty-first century. There were plenty of factual sources of information but little, if any, advice from a knowledgeable and experienced navy spouse. Finally, and perhaps most important, I wanted to express a sense of the challenges and the pleasures of navy life. We really are members of an extended family, and both our triumphs and our occasional tragedies are experiences that deserve to be shared as a community. I tried to do all of these things in the first edition.

Each of these purposes is still valid, but numerous changes occurred in the years since the publication of the first edition. The explosion of electronic information generates an abundance of data that is available to web-connected navy spouses, and I wanted to address how to tap into that pool of knowledge. In addition, communication to our ships, squadrons, submarines, and overseas units is much easier since e-mail emerged as the principal communications path—a vast improvement, with attendant protocols that needed to be discussed. Ashore, navy leadership continues to emphasize the importance of providing quality-of-life improvements to service families, including better housing, child-care, and medical options. The Command Spouse Leadership Course in Newport offers quality advice to command-bound officers and their spouses. Family Service Centers continue to enhance their offerings. Given these changes, virtually all of them beneficial, I wanted to update and expand the second edition to include accurate information for the navy spouses of the new millennium.

There have been great changes operationally, from the composition of the fleet to new deployment patterns. We witnessed military successes in the Balkans and the Persian Gulf, and tragic terrorist attacks such as the one upon USS *Cole*. While these incidents are not the focus of this work, there are consequences for navy spouses. In addition, I also wanted this material published in a less expensive format, so it would be more widely and readily accessible. Hence the quality paperback format that you have in hand, priced at about half of the cost of a hard-cover first edition. I believe the availability of this information at a lower cost should help place it in the hands of many more of our nearly three hundred thousand navy spouses.

Finally, my experiences with the navy expanded. After an additional sea tour with my husband in major command, we made the inevitable cross-country trip to the Pentagon where he worked for the secretary of the navy and then assumed his current position on the staff of the chief of naval operations. It soon became apparent that I could improve upon some of the philosophical advice offered in the first edition. While I certainly don't claim to know all the answers, my sincerest desire has been to provide information, a little wisdom, and some clear resources as you undertake your own voyage of experience and enjoyment with the world's best navy. As my husband would say, Godspeed and open water to you.

Preface to the First Edition

There have been many fine books over the years concerned with helping new navy spouses, many of them published by the Naval Institute Press. Virtually all, however, have been almost exclusively focused on the role of the wives of navy *officers*. They were also written during an era in which the overwhelming majority of navy spouses were female. A great deal has changed in the demographics, role, and character of our navy spouse community over the past decade, and this seemed an opportune time to publish a new book.

With the advent of the all-volunteer navy, we have a far higher percentage of married enlisted sailors. We also have a higher percentage of women in the force, with a commensurately higher number of male spouses. Additionally, the majority of navy spouses work, reflecting the continuing trend in the broad American workforce with an increasing number of dual-income homes.

All of this has led, I believe, to the need for a new book that focuses on the new navy spouse in this emerging era. I have tried to capture the role of the recently arrived navy spouse in today's world while attempting to retain many of the best traditions of earlier days and accommodating the many new trends.

This book is the product not only of my personal experience, but of the help and advice I have received during a lifetime in the navy. Both as a navy junior and a navy spouse, I have been fortunate to learn from many wonderful fellow spouses, both female and male; from officers and enlisted sailors serving all over the navy; from ombudsmen at many different commands; and from many excellent publications. I would particularly like to thank the Naval Services FamilyLine Organization and the Navy Family Service Centers. Naturally, all opinions and errors of fact are my responsibility alone.

My thanks as well to my husband, Jim, and my daughters, Christina and Julia. They all helped by giving Mom time to work on this book, and provided a sounding board on the ideas and opinions expressed throughout.

Finally, I would like to dedicate this book to two perfect naval service spouses: my mother, Mrs. Joan Hall, who spent thirty years "married to the navy" as she followed my father, Capt. Bob Hall, USN (ret.) around the world for many great tours; and my mother-in-law, Shirley Stavridis, who likewise enjoyed a long "career" as a Marine Corps wife, married to Col. George Stavridis, USMC (ret.), my father-in-law. From both of them, I learned to enjoy the travel, adventure, and happiness of life as a navy spouse.

And therein lies my ultimate hope in writing this book—to make your experience as a navy spouse, although certainly challenging at times, enjoyable and meaningful as well.

Laura Stavridis

Navy Spouse's Guide

1
Welcome Aboard

Yea, we go down to sea in ships—
But Hope remains behind,
And Love, with laughter on his lips,
And Peace, of passive mind
                    "At Sea"
                    James Whitcomb Riley

There is a wonderful quality to a life spent in the navy that is difficult
to define. Perhaps it is some combination of the sense of adventure
brought on by moving every few years; the friendships that spring up
among those bound together by their part in one of our nation's greatest and most abiding institutions; the essential feelings of patriotism and
service to country; and, above all, the wonderful sense that you are part
of an organization that genuinely cares about your welfare—a sense of
community that is difficult to find in our increasingly fragmented society.

I grew up in the navy, and I believe in all of its good qualities. This
is not to say that life as a navy spouse will always be easy or without significant challenges: your spouse will be away from you for long periods
of time, there is a certain amount of danger in what a sailor does at sea,
and the pay is not the best. Yet many superb people choose to make the
navy a career, and I believe it is because for most people involved in the
U.S. Navy, at the end of the day the good qualities far outweigh the frustrations and challenges.

My hope in writing this book is to help you, a navy spouse, overcome
those frustrations and challenges and in doing so come to enjoy deeply
your life within the navy community.

Growing up in the Navy

Navy children are referred to as "navy juniors," and I am proud to have
been one. I lived in fifteen different homes between birth and the time
I left college in my early twenties. We were lucky to be stationed overseas twice, both times in Europe, and I enjoyed the experience very
much. We also lived on both U.S. coasts, as far north as Maine and as
far south as Florida. My father was a naval aviator and was deeply

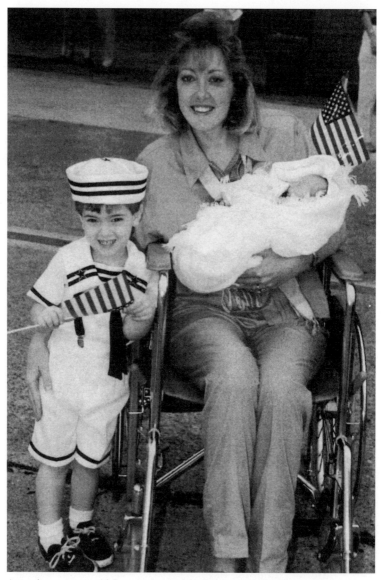

A proud navy spouse with her two navy juniors. U.S. Naval Institute collection.

attached to the navy; my mother was a wonderful navy mom and always made wherever we lived a *home* from our first day in it—whether our abode consisted of a rented apartment, government quarters, or a newly purchased house.

Having enjoyed life as a navy junior, I did not surprise anyone in my family when I married a navy destroyer officer in my early twenties and embarked on a life as a navy spouse. Over the years, I have seen both the good and the challenging days, and I think I have learned a great deal about navy life and how to make it an enjoyable experience, whether you and your sailor plan on a "single hitch" or a full career.

Two Quick Sea Stories

In the course of your association with the navy you will be sure to hear sea stories. This term can mean anything from the "lies and damned lies" that are swapped between sailors about ships on which they have served and commanders they have known, to honest reminiscences passed between acquaintances about times gone by. For our purposes here, I will begin by telling you truthfully about a wonderful navy day, and one that was full of challenges. And I hope by the end of the book you will be prepared to face both kinds of days as well as the far more common ones that lie somewhere in between.

A Really Good Navy Day

My husband's third ship, an Aegis cruiser (don't worry about what that is; we will discuss ship types in chapter 2), was deployed (on overseas duty) in the Indian Ocean—about ten thousand miles from the ship's homeport of San Diego, California. He had been assigned to the ship for over three years, having begun with it in the construction yard (the place the ship was built) in Pascagoula, Mississippi.

After the long years of putting the ship together and training the crew, this first deployment had been very demanding indeed. The schedule had changed several times, and the ship had been sent into the Persian Gulf to escort Kuwaiti tankers through the dangerous Strait of Hormuz, under the noses of Iranian missile batteries. It had been a very anxious and tense deployment, but my husband's battle group (a collection of nearly a dozen ships operating together for mutual support, usually built around an aircraft carrier) had been relieved and was now on its way home in the late summer of 1987.

My husband had orders to transfer back to Washington, D.C., and had to cut the cruise short in order to make his required reporting date at the Pentagon. His relief was on board, the turnover complete, and he received permission from his captain to leave the ship and fly home in order to make it to his next duty station. We had not seen each other in over five months, but he had called me from the ship (we will discuss in chapter 4 how that is possible) and asked me to meet him at the Marriott Hotel in downtown San Diego.

I knew his flight was arriving around six that evening, and I checked into the hotel—making sure we had a great room near the top floor, with all of San Diego spread out below—put on a beautiful dress, and sat in the lobby to await his arrival.

A few minutes past six, a cab pulled up and he got out, still wearing a rumpled set of khakis from the twenty-four-hour series of military flights that had brought him home after nearly six months away. Seeing him walk into that hotel lobby was an ideal conclusion to a perfect navy day. It is hard to describe how wonderful a reunion like that can be, the immense joy of finally being together again—it really is like starting a new life every time it happens. Yes, the separations are long and challenging, but the chance to begin afresh is a magical high that you repeat again and again in a navy life.

A Challenging Navy Day

Now let me share a challenging moment with you, because life as a navy spouse will certainly offer you a few of those as well.

It was in October 1989, as my husband was leaving a tour at the Pentagon, headed back to sea duty as executive officer of a cruiser homeported in Long Beach, California. Because the officer he was relieving had to transfer early, his arrival date had been moved up five months, and most of his "pipeline training" (the schools a sailor attends on the way to a new assignment) was suddenly canceled. We loaded our four-year-old daughter and some pots, pans, and sheets in the car and tore across country, arriving in Los Angeles with exactly twenty-four hours to house hunt before my husband had to jump on a series of flights to meet the ship in Korea.

Los Angeles in the late 1980s was not a pretty place. Earthquakes, riots, smog, and traffic were the four constants. There was no navy housing readily available, and the Navy Lodge was perched on the corner of Highway 405, appropriately named the "Terminal Freeway," and an industrial park by the base. Gang graffiti was sprayed on every other lamppost, and the realtor praised a house she was showing by saying, "The gangs who are in this neighborhood aren't very active at all." Despite our best efforts, we found nothing in our price range in the single day available for house hunting, and my husband was forced to leave us at the Navy Lodge—our reservation running out, with no idea where we would live—and meet the ship for a two-month exercise.

That night I put my four year old to bed in the single room, listened to the traffic whizzing by on the freeway outside the window, and said, "What are we doing in the navy?" As my husband would say, it was not a reenlistment kind of day.

How did it turn out?

As I'm sure you can guess, it all worked out. I was able to call some of the other ship's wives, including the captain's wife, all of whom were very helpful and supportive. The Navy Family Service Center (NFSC) provided me with maps and good general advice about the area. The Navy Lodge extended our reservation. And after about a week of looking diligently, we found a great little house in San Pedro and a wonderful preschool for my daughter.

I will be the first to admit that Los Angeles was not my favorite homeport in my husband's twenty-five-year career; there were many things not to like about the city. But on balance, I'm glad we had a chance to live in the United States' second-largest city and to sample the pulse and energy of a huge multicultural center full of great restaurants, beautiful beaches, and wonderful entertainment opportunities—from the original Disneyland to Knott's Berry Farm to the L.A. County Art Museum.

The message here is simple: life as a navy spouse will be full of amazing highs and deep challenges, almost beyond the understanding of friends and family who are not familiar with such a life. The secret is to savor the highs, and when the challenges come, put your head down, take advantage of all the resources the navy provides for you, and take them on, one at a time. You will be amazed at how skilled you become at overcoming the challenges you meet.

About Those Navy Juniors

As I have mentioned, I grew up a navy junior, and I know firsthand the good and the challenging aspects of being the child of a sailor. But rather than write it myself, in 1996 I asked my sixth-grade daughter, Christina, to capture in a few lines what her eleven years in the navy had been like, and they serve quite well as an introduction to any younger readers. They also offer some insight, for navy spouses, into the navy world as seen through the eyes of a child.

A Few Helpful Hints from a Sixth-Grade Survivor of (Drum Roll) Navy Life as a Kid in the 1990s

Once you get used to one place, what do you have to do when your mom or dad is in the navy? Move, of course. When you finally get friends, what do you have to do? Move, of course. When you finally get your room the way you like it, you have to—you guessed it—move again.

I know all about this, because my dad has been in the navy for twenty years, and that is way more than all of my life. So, almost every two years, I move. But I guess you know all about that, or you wouldn't have bought my mom's book, right?

I have gotten used to it, and there are five simple tips that I use whenever I move. They are about coping with moving or starting at a new school. Here they are:

1. Always try to stay in touch with all the great people you have met or been friends with around the country—so what if your Christmas card list gets a little long? Not to mention that you may live there again.
2. Think ahead about the good things that are part of moving. Try to think of all the new people you are going to meet. Or think about how you are going to arrange your new room. Or about the great new places to go in your new town. This will take your mind off of feeling gloomy about moving. Be positive— it doesn't cost anything and will make you feel lots better.
3. When you get to your new school or neighborhood, try not to talk a lot about "where you used to live." It could make your new friends think you are sorry to have moved to their town (even if you *do* think a lot about your old house and neighborhood).
4. On the first or second day at your new house, be outside a lot. While you are out there, you might see someone your own age. And if you moved in the summertime, you might have a friend to face school with.
5. Here is my final tip: don't be afraid to be really involved where you live now. Sometimes military kids don't want to get involved, because they feel like they will only be there for two or three years. No matter how long you live in a place, you should try to have great friends and be very involved. You'll just end up with lots more friends all over the country as a result.

Finally, is there anyone out there who has never moved? Like kids who are totally new to this navy scene? Well, here are some suggestions (in addition to the ones listed above) that might help you in particular. (And all you "pros" at this moving thing still ought to listen, because you might actually end up staying in one place for more than two years.)

1. Since you have lived in the same house and have had the same friends all of your life, you are probably pretty attached to everyone you know or like in your hometown. On the last days you are at "home," try to make the best of it. For instance, try to see your friends a lot. Exchange addresses and talk about when you will write.
2. Try to help your parents and the movers by staying out of their way and keeping your little brother or sister out of their way also.

3. When you get to your new house, don't sulk in the corners. Or try to be extra mean to your parents (even if there isn't anything else to do). It doesn't make the time go faster, and in fact it only makes you look bad in front of *everyone.*

Well, these are just a few ideas that should help you. Maybe you'll see me on a base somewhere, and remember to have a nice life in . . . the Navy World.

Recently, I asked my ten-year-old daughter to comment for the new millennium.

What It Is Like Being a Navy Kid in the Year 2001

I think being a navy kid is good, but I have to admit there are some bad parts at times.

I have to say that I love having privileges like being able to shop at the base and getting to take tours of ships. But at other times, I really don't like it when my Dad goes away for a long time. I do like it when he comes back from cruises with lots of presents, and we have fun together again. And we learn a lot from his going overseas to lots of foreign countries.

On the subject of moving, I think that is pretty cool—at least when we move to interesting places such as California or Hawaii. But as I said, there are bad parts too like not being able to see my friends anymore or moving in the middle of the school year and having to be new in the class. After we move away from a place, I try to stay in touch with my friends with e-mail and with letters, but it is hard. Maybe when I get older, I'll do better at that. Right now I just try to make new friends really fast by getting on sports teams, taking after-school activities like dance and art classes, and seeing who lives near us. So far that has worked OK, and I've always been able to meet great new friends. You just have to get out there and try.

Overall, I think the navy is pretty cool and I would like to carry on the tradition.

Perspective and a Sense of Humor

The first and most important asset you have in a navy life is a clear sense of perspective. A great deal routinely goes wrong in life: from the flat tire as you are hopping into the car to take your daughter to preschool, to the hot water heater that, with impeccable timing, blows up exactly at the halfway point of any of your spouse's six-month deployments. While these things are never enjoyable at the time, perspective is the quality that allows you to separate the bothersome from the truly life threatening, and permits a balanced approach to events that unfold before you.

The flat tire? Grab a can of Fix-a-Flat (see chapter 4 on emergency road repairs), pump that baby up, and get back on the road. Or call your roadside assistance company (e.g., the American Automobile Association), ask your ship's designated support team member to change the tire, or do it yourself. Hot water heater blew up? Use the Yellow Pages to find someone to repair it. New to the area and unsure who to ask? Call the command ombudsman for some advice, or check with the NFSC, who can steer you to community organizations that monitor business practices in your city.

Perhaps the best tool in your kit is one that we all at times can overlook: a sense of humor. While it may not seem funny when the hot water heater blows up and the water is spreading over the floor of the garage, in the course of your life it is not a true tragedy. You may eventually find yourself telling some friends the story over a glass of wine or a beer at a navy party, complaining that you just cannot figure out how the hot water heater knew, absolutely *knew*, that it was exactly halfway through the deployment. One thing you will certainly develop during your time in the navy is a healthy respect for the malevolent intelligence of appliances, who always know when to self-destruct to inflict the most harm on you. And is there humor in that? Maybe a little.

Serving Your Country

One of the true rewards of being a navy spouse has nothing to do with the excitement of moving, the joys of reunion, or the pleasures in overcoming life's challenges. Instead, it is the pride you will feel in serving your country.

As a navy spouse, you are devoting a great deal of your time and effort to the causes of your country—something you should be aware of and proud about. When your spouse sails to the coast of Haiti as part of an international effort to bring peace and stability to that troubled land, you should be proud. When your spouse's submarine is reported on station in the Persian Gulf during periods of high tension, you should know that the sacrifice of separation is helping keep the peace in a dangerous region where vital U.S. interests are engaged. And when the patrol squadron in which your spouse flies is involved in humanitarian relief efforts in Florida after a major hurricane, flying supplies and experts into the region, you must know that you are very much a part of that important effort.

Your spouse is in the navy in large measure because of a deep and abiding love of country. We are all part of the greatest country in the world, but as a navy spouse you give more to it than almost anyone else. This is well recognized, not only in the navy, but in the larger community as well. Each year, Congress and the president participate in a day recognizing all military spouses for the sacrifices they make and the love they show daily to this beloved land we call the United States of America. Be proud.

The Civilian World

You will be constantly amazed how little your civilian friends know about the military in general and the navy in particular. Among the memorable questions I have heard over twenty years as a navy junior and twenty as a navy spouse:

> The military pays for your housing no matter where you live, right? (Hah)
> Can you get free food at those commissary places? (I wish)
> Do you get to go to sea with your husband if you want to? (Right)
> I guess navy wives are required to be in wives clubs? (Times have changed)
> When his ship is in port, what does he do? Do they just get the time off until they go back to sea again? (I *really* wish)
> I can see what the ships do, but why does the navy need all those bases and buildings? (Let me explain)

You get the idea. While these questions sound ridiculous to those of us who have been navy spouses or navy juniors, they are generally innocent and serve to show the dearth of understanding many (most, actually) civilians have about the armed services.

This lack of knowledge about the military is a growing concern for everyone who studies national security. The United States stopped drafting people into the military in 1972, and the services have been increasingly a career force with less direct input from the civilian world since. Our last major prolonged conflict, the war in Vietnam, ended well over two decades ago. With fewer elected officials who have served in the military, and with the passing of many in the World War II and Korean War generations, there are simply fewer Americans who understand what the military life is all about, especially on the family front.

With the passing of the Cold War and the brief (fortunately successful) Persian Gulf War, the U.S. military has to some degree been relegated to a less prominent role in the national consciousness. Despite the constant strains of frequent major deployments (Bosnia, Haiti, Somalia, Persian Gulf), the success of the military and the seeming ease of its "can do" spirit has led the country to take the military a bit for granted.

And this is where navy spouses come in: to some degree, all of us help portray the navy to the civilian side of society. The image many civilians have of the navy is formed by their impression of the navy spouses they have met as neighbors, friends, and coworkers. We serve as a daily link to the civilian world for our active-duty wives and husbands. Some civilian impressions of the navy—especially what day-to-day life for a navy family is like—are formed through interaction and conversation with *us*.

My advice is always to be honest and forthright about the navy, painting an accurate picture—but, I hope, a very positive one. Just as you would not criticize your family to someone not in it, you should be careful to focus your discussion with civilian friends and neighbors in a positive way on the rewards and the challenges of the service. Let them know that the navy life is full of interesting moments, some great rewards, and many demanding challenges. They will be fascinated, faintly unbelieving, and perhaps quietly envious of the excitement in your life. They will learn that the sacrifices of separation are very demanding, but on the other hand, they will hear that your opportunities to travel and live all over the country and the world are exciting. From you they may learn that your life has a reasonable amount of job security and a solid retirement program, and is populated with many high-quality people.

So be balanced and give your navy a good report card when you talk to those civilians.

A Part of the Team

You are a part of the best team in the world: the U.S. Navy. In over two hundred years we may have lost a few battles, but we have never been defeated in a war at sea. As Secretary of Defense William Perry said in early 1996 (when navy ships and aircraft stepped in between Taiwan and China to maintain peace in Asia), "We have the best damned navy in the world." Our flag has never been driven from the oceans of this earth, and our ships, submarines, and aircraft are on station, standing guard, twenty-four hours a day, every day of the year.

As a navy spouse, you are an enormous part of the navy's ability to perform its abiding mission: the conduct of prompt and sustained combat operations at sea. Without your love and support, the nearly three hundred thousand married active-duty navy personnel could not perform their demanding jobs at sea or in the air throughout the world. For the remainder of this book, I hope to give you the kind of down-to-earth, real-world advice that will truly make your time in the navy the best and most memorable voyage of your life.

Three Cheers for a Navy Spouse

A true navy spouse is someone who

owns three dozen sets of drapes, but none that fit the new bedroom window

knows how to load a van with three kids, a dog, two cats, a hamster, and six suitcases and drive across country, all in less than a week

has checked into the Navy Lodge in Pearl Harbor only to discover the household goods were moved to Mayport

has children born in three different states

finds it a little suspicious when a family member sees the same doctor twice in a row

knows the best time to go commissary shopping in both Norfolk and San Diego

has actually heard of Adak, Alaska

instinctively shows a military ID card when entering Wal-Mart

knows how to fit ten rooms of furniture into a six-room apartment.

2
Getting Under Way

Take in all lines . . . starboard engine back one third; port engine ahead one
third; right full rudder . . . rudder amidships; all back one third.
Traditional initial commands for getting a destroyer under way
when tied up starboard side to the pier. *Knights Modern Seamanship*

Just as the captain of a navy ship needs to know how to get the ship
away from the pier and headed out to sea, you—as a navy spouse—need
to understand some very basic and traditional aspects of the navy. Without at least a simple knowledge of your sailor's organization and career,
much of what comes home from the ship, squadron, or shore command
will sound very confusing indeed. Like any other large organization, particularly one with over two hundred years of tradition behind it, the
navy has a unique culture and structure. In this chapter we will cover
some of the basic elements of your navy. I hope that when you finish
reading this, much of what you hear and read about ranks, rates, ships,
squadrons, bases, and all other elements of the navy's organization and
structure will sound more familiar. After a few years as a navy spouse,
you can be sure it will all become very clear.

A Brief History of the Navy

Founded on 13 October 1775, the Continental Navy began with Congress authorizing the outfitting of two vessels with ten guns each for
cruising against British ships. Throughout the Revolution, the early
American navy played a significant role, both in attacking British warships and merchant vessels and in assisting the Continental Army in
land operations. Interestingly, the first submarine operations occurred
during the Revolution with a very primitive submersible boat called the
Turtle.

By 1778, the first official salute (the firing of a gun as a token of respect) to the new American navy was executed in Quiberon Bay on
France's Atlantic coast to a ship commanded by John Paul Jones, who
would emerge as the most famous naval hero of the Revolutionary War.
His greatest engagement was the capture of the British frigate HMS *Se-*

rapis by his ship, the *Bonhomme Richard,* after the British had demanded that he surrender, and to which he uttered, "I have not yet begun to fight." Another great Revolutionary War naval hero was Capt. John Barry of Philadelphia, who received the first commission in the United States Navy. Both John Paul Jones and John Barry are considered the "fathers" of the American navy.

In the early 1800s, the U.S. Navy engaged in several memorable battles with Barbary pirates from North Africa in the Mediterranean Sea, including famous attacks by Commo. Edward Preble and Capt. Stephen Decatur. During the War of 1812, the U.S. fleet consisted of only seventeen seaworthy ships, compared to the Royal Navy's fleet of well over one thousand. As a result of this disparity, the American fleet was used—as it was during the Revolution—for commerce raiding (attacking merchant ships) and support to the army ashore. One famous battle in 1813 occurred between HMS *Shannon* and the American *Chesapeake,* in which the *Chesapeake*'s captain, James Lawrence, said with his dying breath, "Don't give up the ship" as he was carried below in the heat of battle, mortally wounded. Other heroes of the War of 1812 include Commos. John Rodgers and Oliver Hazard Perry, and Capt. David Porter. Despite the United States's loss in the war, the navy was well regarded for its courageous fight against overwhelming odds.

During the Civil War, both the North and the South had formidable navies. The South was noted for its daring commerce raiding, with the "war cruises" of the *Alabama* under Capt. Ralphael Semmes being the most outstanding. The North confined itself to conducting an extensive blockade (preventing merchant ships from entering ports) of the South and supporting the army ashore in a wide variety of battles. One of the most well-known encounters was between two of the first "iron-clad" ships (those with steel hulls)—the South's *Merrimack* (renamed the *Virginia*) and the North's *Monitor.* The battle, although inconclusive, was the first ever fought between iron-clad ships. One renowned naval hero of the Civil War was Adm. David Farragut, who said, "Damn the torpedoes. Full speed ahead" at the battle of Mobile Bay, Alabama.

In the late 1800s, the navy had an intellectual renaissance, led by distinguished strategists Capt. Alfred Thayer Mahan and Adm. Stephen B. Luce. Also during this period, the Naval War College was founded in Newport, Rhode Island, and the navy played an important role in the Spanish-American War, which was ignited by the sinking of the battleship *Maine* in Havana harbor in a mysterious explosion. The most important naval battle of that conflict was fought on the other side of the world, in the Spanish colony of the Philippines, when Commo. George Dewey led his Asiatic Squadron into Manila Bay under cover of darkness and opened fire with the words, "You may fire when ready, Gridley" to the captain of his flagship, *Olympia*. Dewey went on to become a famous admiral and naval hero. Another important event of the Spanish-American War occurred when the Atlantic Fleet also destroyed Spain's fleet in the Battle of Santiago, Cuba.

By the turn of the century, the United States had a strong navy, including its first modern submarine, the *Holland*. President Theodore Roosevelt was a significant supporter of the navy's expansion, sending the so-called "Great White Fleet" of major warships on a worldwide cruise. In the years leading up to World War I, the navy was very active throughout the world, especially in the Caribbean. Cdr. Robert Peary, of the navy's Civil Engineer Corps, was the first man to reach the North Pole, where he raised the American flag. By 1911 the navy was very involved in aviation, and Lt. T. Gordon Ellyson became the navy's first pilot.

The sinking of the British liner *Lusitania* (with many Americans on board) by a German U-boat (a commerce-raiding submarine) helped spur American entry into World War I in 1917. During the war, U.S. Navy destroyers attacked and sank many German submarines, escorted convoys to Europe, and supported the battle ashore in a variety of ways.

In the years between the two world wars, the navy was drastically reduced in size along with the rest of the armed forces. The attack on Pearl Harbor on 7 December 1941 caught the entire nation and the U.S. Pacific Fleet by surprise and resulted in the loss of many heavy battleships. World War II was the greatest chapter in the U.S. Navy's history, and from 1941 through 1945 the American fleet grew to an overpowering size, with thousands of warships. By the end of the numerous battles in both the Atlantic and Pacific, the U.S. Navy was the dominant force on the world's seas—a position it holds today.

World War II gave the navy its greatest heroes, including four Fleet Admirals (five-star rank, unused today): Chester Nimitz (Pacific Fleet commander), Ernest King (Chief of Naval Operations), William "Bull" Halsey (slashing attacker and carrier commander), and William Leahy (advisor to President Franklin D. Roosevelt). Two other memorable World War II leaders were the quiet, studious, and effective Adm. Raymond Spruance and Commo. Arleigh "31 Knot" Burke, the superb destroyer squadron commander.

The key contributions of the U.S. Navy during World War II involved defeating and bottling up the navies of Germany, Japan, and Italy; destroying the German and Japanese submarine threat; securing the use of the seas for Allied invasions of the European continent and the island chains of the Pacific; and blockading the enemy powers, thereby eventually strangling their economies.

The Cold War lasted from about 1945 through the collapse of the

Soviet Union in 1991. During this time, the navy was involved in a wide variety of combat and near-combat activities all over the world, including the Korean War, the Cuban missile crisis, the Vietnam War, and the Persian Gulf War. Navy ships, submarines, and aircraft were "on station" all over the world, deterring the Soviet Union from attempting to expand their influence or start a larger conflict with the United States or our allies.

Today, the navy is focused on contributing to U.S. national security throughout the world, from the Balkans to the Persian Gulf. It appears that the world has grown more complicated and dangerous since the end of the Cold War, and the navy is at the forefront of many trouble spots, defending U.S. citizens (e.g., diplomats in endangered embassies), protecting vital raw materials needed by our economy (such as oil from the Persian Gulf), and deterring would-be aggressors (e.g., Iraq's Saddam Hussein and North Korea's Kim Il Sung) from attacking our allies. In recent years, the navy has launched many Tomahawk and aircraft strikes against terrorists as well, most recently in Afghanistan.

Navy Organization and Mission

Just what, exactly, is the organization of the navy?

First, the Department of the Navy (sometimes abbreviated DoN) is only a part (along with the Departments of the Army and Air Force) of the larger Department of Defense (DoD). The secretary of defense, or "SecDef," works directly for the president, who is the commander in chief of all U.S. armed forces. Below the president and the secretary of defense, who are called the National Command Authorities (NCA), is the chairman of the Joint Chiefs of Staff. This four-star officer is chosen from one of the four armed forces and is the senior uniformed individual in the DoD.

The Department of the Navy includes both the navy *and* the Marine Corps. While the focus of this book is entirely on the navy itself, we should always remember that we are part of a U.S. Navy–Marine Corps *team* and of an overall navy department.

The Department of the Navy is headed by a senior civilian, the secretary of the navy. He or she is appointed by the president, confirmed by the Senate, and works directly for the secretary of defense. The next senior official is also a civilian, the undersecretary of the navy.

Below the secretary—senior to all navy admirals—is the chief of naval operations. Abbreviated "CNO," this is the senior uniformed officer in the Department of the Navy, and he or she works directly for the secretary of the navy on all issues. The comparable officer in the Marine Corps is the commandant. A staff of over two thousand dedicated professionals work for the secretary of the navy and the CNO in the Pentagon in Washington, D.C. They are charged with "organizing, training, and equipping" the navy. Below the CNO is a vice chief of naval operations, or VCNO, and below that officer are the many other admirals (called flag officers) in the chain of command. The mission of the navy is quite simple: to be prepared to conduct prompt combat operations at sea. Everyone in the navy directs their efforts toward that end.

Below the Washington chain of command comes the rest of the navy, broadly termed "the fleet." When someone says "the fleet," they mean virtually everyone involved in or directly supporting operations at sea. This encompasses the majority of the uniformed officers, chiefs, and sailors in the navy. Let's talk about them first, because if you don't understand the fleet, you will never understand the navy.

Operational Navy Structure—"The Fleet"

Operationally, the fleet is divided into two large entities, the commander in chief of the Pacific Fleet and the commander in chief of the Atlantic Fleet. Below that come many subordinate commands, including the "type commanders," who manage surface ships, submarines, and aircraft—for example, commander, Naval Surface Forces, U.S. Atlantic Fleet (quite a mouthful). Your sailor will use the term "SURFLANT" when referring to this level. It is important to know that this is very high in the chain of command, generally where inspection teams come from, so you may hear it mentioned.

Ships, Submarines, Squadrons

The most basic element in the navy's fleet organization is the ship, submarine, or squadron. When sailors talk about a ship, they generally mean a surface ship (one that sails on the surface of the ocean). Although a submarine is a specialized type of ship, in conversation it is normally referred to as a sub or, affectionately, a boat. *Never* make the mistake of calling your sailor's surface ship a boat—to a surface sailor, a boat is either one of the small craft associated with the ship (a motor whaleboat, gig, or launch, for example) or a submarine. Finally, squadrons are groups of aircraft of similar type, with the associated naval aviators, maintenance, and support personnel.

As a general rule, all three—ships, submarines, and squadrons—are commanded by either a commander (O-5) or captain (O-6). While in command, a commander is called "Captain" as a courtesy on both surface ships and submarines; in a squadron, the commanding officer is normally referred to as "Skipper" or as the CO, but never as the captain.

Some types of smaller ships (e.g., patrol craft and minesweepers) are commanded by more junior officers, including both lieutenants and lieutenant commanders. As a courtesy, they, too, are called "Captain" while in command. When they leave command, they are again referred to by their rank. There are roughly three hundred ships and submarines in the navy and about ninety squadrons. These numbers may decrease somewhat as the final round of post–Cold War budget cuts and downsizing moves are completed, but they should remain fairly stable for the next decade, at least.

The operational navy is mainly organized around joint task forces, which generally include an aircraft carrier and the associated airwing; several large amphibious ships; a group of four to six surface combatants, including cruisers, destroyers, and frigates; two attack submarines; one or two support ships carrying fuel and ammunition; some special operations contingents; and support from the other services as required, including air force land-based aircraft, army helicopters and troops, and so forth.

As a navy spouse, you might want to have a very basic level of operational knowledge about each of these main components—after all, the entire navy is focused on preparing them and sending them forward on deployments.

Aircraft Carrier

This is a very large and expensive surface ship with over five thousand men and women assigned when the airwing is embarked—truly a city at sea. The chance to see a carrier is always worth a tour. The associated airwing, which has about eighty planes and can launch strikes and attacks thousands of miles ashore, is the heart of the navy's striking capability.

Amphibious Ships

There are several types of "amphibs," as they are called. Their role is to carry marines and their equipment to forward-deployed areas and put them ashore to defend American interests, rescue stranded U.S. citizens, support United Nations missions, and perform myriad other tasks—from humanitarian missions to noncombatant evacuations. While somewhat slow and not well armed, amphibs carry a potent punch in the form of the U.S. Marines.

Cruisers, Destroyers, and Frigates

Heir to the richest traditions of naval combat at sea, many of these "greyhounds of the fleet" carry the accurate and long-range (one thousand miles) Tomahawk cruise missile as their primary offensive punch (most cruisers and destroyers, but not frigates). All three carry many surface-to-air missiles to defend our ships from enemy attack, as well as torpedoes to strike enemy submarines and helicopters for scouting and other missions. They are very fast and well armed, and highly sought after as duty for surface sailors. You will hear the word "Aegis" (which means "shield" in Greek) used in the context of some of the cruisers and destroyers; it means that the sophisticated and capable Aegis combat system (with the best sensors, computers, and display equipment) is embarked.

Support Ships

There is a wide variety of these important ships, which supply the fleet with fuel, ammunition, spare and repair parts, and food on distant stations. Some are highly specialized and many are quite high tech. Their primary role is to conduct underway replenishments—an at-sea operation wherein a receiving ship pulls up alongside (while both ships continue in the same direction) and receives the support items across the water from a distance of about 150 feet. This is quite a sight, and somewhat dangerous, but it's done every day.

Submarines

These submersible ships are nuclear powered (they never need gas) and very silent under the water. They come in two types: attack submarines and fleet ballistic missile submarines. They almost never operate on the surface, instead working "at depth" (well under two hundred feet and often far deeper), where they execute a wide variety of missions—from launching ballistic or Tomahawk cruise missiles to scouting for enemy ships and sinking them with torpedoes. In recent years, the attack submarines have come to operate far more frequently with the joint task forces. The ballistic missile boats work independently, staying at depth throughout their ninety-day patrols and providing a solid deterrent to any opponent considering an attack on the United States.

Aviation Squadrons

Naval aviation is extremely rich in its variety of aircraft and squadrons. Some of the most important are:

- Sea-based aircraft: fighter and attack aircraft (F-14, F/A-18, F/A-18E/F, and EA-6) operate from the deck of the aircraft carrier and provide its offensive punch and defensive counterair ability. Antisubmarine and antisurface aircraft include both fixed-wing (S-3B) and helicopter

(SH-60). The carrier also carries air early warning aircraft (E-2C) and a variety of other electronic and support aircraft. Other ships—including cruisers, destroyers, frigates, support ships, and amphibs—carry various kinds of helicopters for both combat and support functions.

- Land-based aircraft: long-range patrol aircraft (P-3) and many other types of support and communications aircraft are land based—although their missions find them operating almost exclusively over the oceans and littorals of the world in direct support of naval forces.

Special Operations

The navy also has a small but important segment of its operational capability invested in special operations—the famous Sea-Air-Land (SEALs), small boat units, coastal patrol craft, and other units. They operate in support of the navy and all other services in a wide variety of operations. If your spouse is involved in special operations, he or she is an exceptional person indeed and faces many challenging and exciting missions. Contrary to what you might see in the movies, these missions are almost never "wild and crazy." Instead, they are the most carefully planned and deliberately executed of all naval missions. While they carry a certain amount of danger due to the high degree of challenge involved, each individual receives extensive training, and they are a superbly motivated group.

Other Support Organizations—Service to the Fleet

Throughout the Department of the Navy, there are many organizations that provide support to the fleet, and your sailor may work at one someday or be involved with them from a professional perspective. These organizations include the staff of the CNO in Washington (often called the OPNAV staff); the various systems commands (e.g., Naval Sea Systems Command) in Washington and elsewhere that provide engineering and material support to the fleet; naval districts throughout the United States that oversee bases; and of course the naval bases themselves. The key naval complexes in the United States include Norfolk, Virginia; San Diego, California; Pearl Harbor, Hawaii; Kings Bay, Georgia; Jacksonville and Pensacola, Florida; Groton, Connecticut; Bremerton, Everett, and Whidbey Island, Washington; Great Lakes, Illinois; Memphis, Tennessee; Ingleside, Texas; Newport, Rhode Island; and Annapolis, Maryland. Ships are homeported overseas in Yokosuka and Sasebo, Japan; Gaeta, Italy; and Bahrain in the Persian Gulf.

An excellent reference guide for a navy spouse is the annual "Guide to U.S. Military Installations," which is a supplement to *Navy Times*. It lists all military bases (not just navy, but Marine Corps, army, air force, and coast guard as well) throughout the United States and overseas. Similar guidebooks can be purchased at most exchanges. It is a valuable tool when you are looking ahead to a transfer or when traveling on vacation or during transfers, because it lists all facilities at each base. In the resources section of this book, you will find a long and detailed list of excellent publications that can be very helpful.

Carrier Battle Groups and Amphibious Readiness Groups

Carrier Battle Groups (CVBG)

Most sailors will be assigned to either a carrier battle group or an amphibious readiness group while they are on sea duty, so it seems worthwhile to provide a little background on how each is organized. A carrier battle group is comprised of eight to ten ships centered on one of the United States's twelve aircraft carriers and is identified by the name of the aircraft carrier, for instance, *Abraham Lincoln* Battle Group or *George Washington* Battle Group. Each carrier battle group is commanded by a rear admiral, who has a staff of about seventy navy personnel to help him run a battle group consisting of four to six cruisers, destroyers, and frigates; one or two submarines; and one supply ship. Onboard the carrier will be an airwing with about eighty aircraft. There will be a captain in command of the airwing and another captain (called a commodore) who is in charge of the surface ships. There are many navy personnel in each battle group and to give you a sense of the size, the estimated numbers are in table 2.1.

Table 2.1. Estimated Carrier Battle Group Census for 2001

	Officers	Additional Personnel
Admiral's staff	25	35
Carrier:	150	3,000
Airwing	130	1,500
Cruisers and destroyers	25	360
Frigates	18	200
Submarine	15	130
Supply ship	40	680

Source: U.S. Navy

Table 2.2. Estimated Amphibious Readiness Group Census for 2001

	U.S. Navy	U.S. Marine Corps
LHD/LHA	1,000	2,000
LPD	425	900
LSD	350	300

Source: U.S. Navy

Amphibious Readiness Group (ARG)

An amphibious readiness group is an assembly of amphibious ships organized to support assault operations of the U.S. Marines launched from ships by either small boats or aircraft. There are generally three or four ships in an amphibious readiness group, including either a large-deck *Tarawa*-class general purpose assault ship (LHA) or *Wasp*-class multipurpose assault ship (LHD). Like the carrier battle groups, the amphibious readiness group is known by the name of the largest ship, for example, the *Boxer* ARG.

The amphibious squadron commander, generally a navy captain, is in command of the amphibious readiness group. The Marine Corps is led by a Marine Expeditionary Unit (MEU) commander, who is a full colonel. The two work together to plan and execute operations that will move the marines ashore.

In addition to the large-deck LHA or LHD, there are also dock landing ships (LSDs) of the *Whidbey Island* and *Harper's Ferry* class. Soon the new LPD-17 *San Antonio*–class transport dock will be joining the fleet. Together, these ships will transport the marines and all of their combat equipment and vehicles. They will also embark a wing of marine aircraft, including six Super Cobra attack helicopters (AH-1W), twenty-four combat assault and cargo helicopters (CH-46), and approximately ten other heavy-lift and ship-to-shore utility helicopters (CH-53 and UH-1N). At times, the amphibious readiness group also will deploy with the sophisticated AV-8B Harrier aircraft, a fixed-wing airplane that can take off and land vertically if necessary. The marines can move ashore either by air assault or by landing craft air cushions (LCAC), high speed water and land vehicles launched from the amphibious readiness group ships.

Like the carrier battle groups, there are many navy (and marine) personnel in each amphibious readiness group (table 2.2). The numbers are approximate.

Size of the Navy

The navy has been declining in size over the past decade, as the post–Cold War budget cuts have had an impact on overall size. In 1986, for example, there were 72,000 officers and just over 500,000 enlisted men and women. By 1995, those numbers had been cut to about 59,000 officers and 370,000 enlisted men and women. This decline was mirrored in "force structure" (the number of ships, submarines, and aircraft) and "infrastructure" (support bases and shore support facilities). Since then, we have generally steadied at these levels.

Despite shrinking overall, we still have a very significant number of navy spouses and children: over 240,000 spouses, and about 400,000 children, most of whom are five to twelve years old. Nearly 60 percent of our enlisted men and women are married, as are almost 70 percent of the officer corps.

While numbers may decrease in the years ahead, most navy officials believe the drawdown in personnel is largely over, so our total numbers should remain fairly stable over the next decade. A large-scale military operation such as the war on terrorism may change this.

"BuPers" and Your "Detailer"

Perhaps the most important shore support organization from your perspective as a navy spouse is the Bureau of Naval Personnel, or "BuPers." Often referred to simply as "the bureau," it is headed by a three-star admiral and controls all aspects of the navy personnel system. It is in charge of arranging for orders that send hundreds of thousands of sailors all over the world; arranging and facilitating the all-important promotion boards that establish professional advancements; setting up policies that affect the quality of life of sailors and their families; and ensuring that "the system" is fair, open, and well managed.

You will often hear your spouse talk about "the detailer." The detailer works at the bureau and is in charge of coordinating assignments for a set group of navy people. For example, if your spouse is a second class gunner's mate, she may be detailed by a first class petty officer (normally also a gunner's mate) or even a chief petty officer. If your spouse is a captain, he will be detailed by a senior captain. Both the first class petty officer and the senior captain who work at the bureau do essentially the same thing: represent your spouse in the negotiation for orders.

While detailers don't always provide the exact set of orders desired (and are therefore sometimes castigated in the fleet), they are—by and large—a fair-minded, hard-working group who seek to balance the needs of the navy with the needs, desires, and career requirements of the individual.

"Goodbye, Lieutenant Commander Mom." U.S. Naval Institute collection.

Assignments—Afloat and Ashore

The detailer will work with your spouse to provide "orders," which will assign your sailor either to an afloat or an ashore command. Duty afloat will be challenging, and the majority of this book will be devoted to how you can successfully be the spouse of a navy sailor assigned to sea duty.

Sea duty tours generally last from two to four years and will include one or two forward deployments (of up to six months) in that time. We will talk in depth about coping with deployments later in the book. While your spouse is on sea duty, be prepared for him or her to be out to sea a good deal of the time, perhaps well over 50 percent of the tour. Navy personnel may also have "duty days" where their presence is required overnight on the ship or submarine, even though it is in port. This may be difficult to understand—after all, not very many other professions consistently require that spouses spend the night at the "office"—but it is necessary to protect and safeguard the ships and their complex systems from fire, flooding, or sabotage.

When your spouse completes duty with the operational navy—in a ship, submarine, squadron, or special operations unit—it is time to "come ashore," as we say in the navy. The good news is that you will generally see a great deal more of your spouse when he or she is on shore duty; the bad news is that you may miss the camaraderie and social life experienced by spouses whose sailors are on sea duty. You will find that sea duty—with its separations—tends to draw the spouses together more than shore duty. On balance, both sea duty and shore duty have their good and challenging days. The nice thing about the navy is that you can switch back and forth—so you never become bored with the same pattern in life.

Shore duty can occur in a wide variety of settings. One common situation is assignment to a large navy base, which is—in some ways—like being part of a ship again. Like a ship, the base has a defined mission, very dedicated people working toward that mission, and a similar chain of command and structure. A base has a CO, an executive officer (XO, second in command), department heads, division officers—everything you became used to on sea duty. The difference, of course, is that a base does not get under way.

Another common shore duty assignment is to a training command. These interesting and challenging assignments are located all over the country and involve training the navy team. Or your sailor may be a student and find him- or herself ashore attending courses that can last as long as a year—from advanced sonar training for an enlisted technician to the Naval War College for midgrade to senior officers (O-4 to O-6).

Related to training is recruiting, or bringing new people into the navy. While very rewarding, recruiting involves long hours and can be very challenging shore duty. Your sailor will need to be an outgoing and organized individual to succeed as a recruiter. General duty on a large staff, either in Washington, D.C., or at one of the major naval centers (Norfolk, San Diego, Pearl Harbor), is also a possibility.

The key to enjoying shore duty is to bring the same level of enthusiasm that you displayed while your sailor was on sea duty. Be sure to savor the more frequent presence of your spouse, and work hard to take advantage of having your sailor home from the sea. Involvement with navy activities (wardroom and ship's parties, spouses groups) will still be available, but you may choose to be somewhat less involved since your sailor is around a good deal more.

Chain of Command

"Chain of command" is an expression you will hear endlessly while your spouse serves in the navy. Essentially, it means the people for whom your sailor works (who are "up" the chain of command) and those who work for your sailor (who are "down" the chain of command). Visualize this: a long, unbroken chain of administrative authority that runs from the president of the United States at the top, through the secretary of defense, down past the secretary of the navy and chief of naval operations, through the fleet commanders and type commanders, and into the ship, squadron, or submarine where your spouse works. But the chain does not stop there. Far from it. It then proceeds from the CO of your spouse's unit, through the XO, department head, and division officer, and down through the leading chief petty officer. Then there is normally a leading petty officer (an E-6), and then perhaps section leaders, squad leaders, or some other level of authority. Ultimately, the chain of command ends with the most junior seaman, airman, corpsman, or other junior person in the unit.

The beauty of the chain of command is its simplicity and elegance. It truly flows in a straight line up from the most junior people to the most senior. Everyone knows where they are in the chain and how to interact with those junior and senior to them.

Your sailor will be very careful to respect the chain of command, ensuring that any requests, ideas, commands, or other forms of communication stay "in the chain." For example, suppose your sailor is a division officer (a job) and an ensign (a rank of O-1) on a destroyer. Up the chain of command is a lieutenant (O-3) department head; just below your sailor is the leading chief petty officer (both a rank, E-7, and a job within the division). When requests come up from the men and women in the division, they will be routed through the leading chief petty officer, and not simply placed on your spouse's (the division officer's) desk; likewise, when the department head wants to pass some direction along to the division, the lieutenant department head will pass it through your spouse (the division officer). All communication (in almost every situation, except an emergency or some other unique case) will be passed through the chain of command. It is the glue that holds the fabric of the navy together.

Ranks and Rates

Since this topic is fundamental, the odds are good that you already have some appreciation of it, but here is a simple reference: the navy is divided into officer and enlisted groups. The enlisted rates are designated as E-1 through E-9; officers' ranks are O-1 through O-10. There is also a small group of warrant officers (W-1 through W-4)—former enlisted men and women who have obtained a commission—as well as midshipmen, who are the most junior commissioned officers and who rank between a W-1 and a W-2. At the pinnacle of the enlisted rate structure is the master chief petty officer of the navy, who wears a special third star over his or her "crow"; at the top of the officer ranks is the Fleet Admiral, who wears a fifth star, although no such individual is currently appointed.

There is a distinction between rank, rate, and rating that is worth mentioning, since they are often confused in conversation. The rank or rate is the level or pay grade an individual has attained; for example, E-5 is a rate of second class petty officer, and O-3 is a rank of lieutenant. A rating applies only to enlisted men and women and indicates their occupational specialty, as in a yeoman (a clerk) or a gunner's mate (specialist in shooting ordnance), for example. Each rating among enlisted men and women has a symbol or insignia that sets it apart and is worn on the uniform.

In the officer ranks, there are not only *line* officers (who are qualified for command at sea and ashore), but *staff corps* officers as well (who may command within their respective specialties, but can never command a ship or a naval station). Examples of the latter include civil engineer, supply, chaplain, medical, medical service, dental, and nurse corps officers. There are also special duty officers in such areas as naval intelligence, engineering duty, law, public affairs, and so forth. They can command ashore, but not at sea. Finally, both line and staff corps officers may be designated limited duty officers (generally former enlisted men and women) in certain technical fields (electronics, operations, ordnance, etc.).

Uniforms

Uniforms are at the heart of any military organization. Wearing them allows everyone to see instantly the grade of an individual; it also promotes uniformity of response and reaction and generally bonds an organization—all important attributes for success in the high stress and constant change of combat operations.

While a detailed discussion of uniforms is beyond our scope here, there are several things you as a navy spouse should be aware of about your sailor's uniforms. First, encourage your spouse to take pride and care in wearing them; part of his or her evaluation will be based on appearance in uniform. Help your spouse prepare his or her uniform for work if you have time, and don't let your sailor out the door if he or she is not in a proper, clean, and well-fitting uniform. Second, uniforms, while somewhat expensive, are actually less costly than civilian clothes for most comparable job settings. They are also generally easy to care for today, largely made of wash-and-wear fabrics. Certain uniforms (service dress blues, for example) will have to be dry-cleaned, but most uniforms, both officer and enlisted, can be suitably cleaned and pressed at home. Third, take pride in your spouse's uniform. Go out to dinner with him or her in uniform once in awhile—you may be surprised at the positive response you receive.

Reenlistment

Reenlistment applies only to enlisted sailors, but it is one of the most traditional acts of the service. It is a contractual pledge, executed in writing following administration of a sworn oath, that commits your sailor to a specified period of service in the navy. These periods can be as little as two years or as long as six, and there is discussion about instituting a longer ten-year reenlistment. Sometimes, a reenlistment comes with a bonus (the selective reenlistment bonus, or SRB), normally paid over the course of the enlistment period in annual sums.

Depending on your spouse's particular occupational skills, he or she may be eligible for up to $60,000 for remaining in the service. On the other hand, if your sailor is in a crowded career field, he or she may simply reenlist for "the benefits of rate," as the expression goes. The SRB is calculated using a complicated formula that includes time in service, rank, need for the skills, and length of the commitment. The career counselor at your sailor's command will calculate the bonus, but you should be aware of it and prepare to invest it wisely. Half of the bonus can be paid upon the reenlistment, and the other half can be divided into equal payments given at the start of each year of the new enlistment. If your spouse reenlists in the Persian Gulf, there are significant tax benefits. Have your spouse see the career counselor for details.

Reenlistment ceremonies should be big events, and you should attend as an important part of the navy team. Normally, you will be awarded a certificate and be recognized by your spouse's CO. Some commands even present flowers to the female spouses.

Pay

When thinking about navy pay, it is easy to envision the old image of a paymaster sitting behind a battered wooden desk, with a long line of sailors in front of him, counting out money the night before the ship pulls into Shanghai harbor—a scene right out of the old movie *The Sand Pebbles*. Nothing could be further from today's high-tech, computerized world of direct deposit (each month, money is deposited automatically into your designated checking account) and automated tellers (money machines) on board most ships. But let's take a look at the broad background of the navy pay system.

As opposed to the civilian world, where an individual draws a single flat-rate salary, in the navy your sailor will receive a sometimes confusing variety of different types of compensation—up to thirty different types of allowances and fifty types of special payments, for example.

First and most important is "base pay." This is the fundamental portion of pay and can be quickly ascertained by examining any current pay chart. As you can see, basic pay is determined based on two criteria: time in service and pay grade. As your sailor moves along in both categories, there will be normal increases in base pay. It is also a portion of your pay that is taxed, through normal withholding procedures, by the federal government.

Two common allowances (which are not taxed) are the basic allowance for housing (BAH) and the basic allowance for subsistence (BAS). These allowances are based not on time in service, but on pay grade and other factors. The former helps with housing costs; the latter with food. BAH varies based on the number of dependents, the quality of housing offered, and whether the spouse is also in the service. It is important to know that when you live in base housing, you generally forfeit your BAH. The only exception is if the housing is deemed substandard. Since utilities are paid by the government in base housing, living there is normally a positive financial situation. Most often, there are not enough housing units on base to accommodate all families who want them, although there have been gains in this important quality-of-life issue over the past few years. As for BAS, this is a payment made if your sailor is not eating at government expense—that is, at the base galley (cafeteria) or on the ship or submarine. There are several levels of BAS, and your sailor's disbursing office can ensure that your family is receiving the correct amount. Remember, the purpose of BAS is not to feed the family, but to provide three meals each day for the sailor.

Every year, by law, there is a pay raise for navy personnel. Sometimes these raises focus on base pay, while other years the focus is on the allowances. These increases have ranged from fairly significant increases (8–10 percent) in the early 1980s as the Reagan administration sought to make up for years of neglect, to moderate increases in more recent years. In 1996, for example, there was a 2.4 percent pay raise in basic pay and BAS and a 5.2 percent increase in BAH. In 2001, the pay raise was 3.7 percent of base pay, with other targeted increases. Increases generally are set by subtracting one percentage point from an annual index of private sector (nongovernment) wage growth. As a general observation, military pay lags behind comparable wages in the private sector, but there is some compensation in the relatively generous retirement system, the steady pay grade increases, regular seniority increases, and somewhat better job security than found in civilian jobs.

In addition to basic pay, BAH, and BAS, there are many different types of special allowances. Special allowances include travel payments when you execute a move, including per diem (daily) payments for food and housing in between; transportation expenses when moving; dislocation allowances to help during moves with extra BAH payments; temporary lodging allowances (TLAs) for overseas moves; and temporary lodging expenses (TLEs) for stateside moves. (We will discuss these in more detail in chapter 6.)

There are also family separation allowances (FSAs) for families undergoing lengthy separations. For example, a sailor on a six-month deployment (or any separation over thirty days) would receive a payment of one hundred dollars each month.

In addition to basic pay and allowances, there are many different types of specialty pays (over fifty), ranging from hazardous duty to flight pay to reenlistment bonuses. There are, for example, special pays for controlling aircraft, speaking a foreign language, and serving at sea. This is a complicated and detail-oriented segment of the navy's compensation plan, and it can—and often does—change from year to year. If your sailor is in an occupational specialty that qualifies, full information is available from your disbursing office. You need to remember that specialty pays can disappear when your sailor's status changes—the most obvious example being the shift from sea duty to shore duty, which can suddenly decrease total pay by hundreds of dollars each month.

The bottom line in these pay issues is simple: stay informed and make sure your sailor works closely with the disbursing office. This means reading the monthly leave and earning statements (LESs) and keeping them on file, reading books like *Navy Spouse's Guide,* and checking out *Navy Times,* which is an excellent source of information on current financial matters that affect navy families. When you have questions, write them down and have your sailor obtain answers from the disbursing office. They will be glad to provide information. Your NFSC is also a good source of general information on financial matters.

Promotions

One of the most fundamental elements of military life is the highly structured scale of ranks that runs from the youngest, newest seaman to the most senior four-star admiral. Within the navy, you will find that people are very concerned with promotions, particularly since the navy has an "up or out" system of advancement. This means that an individual must continue to be promoted or will be eventually separated.

The conditions and circumstances vary, but the basic up or out element of the system is employed to ensure that the navy's population remains young, energetic, and active—all attributes necessary for an organization whose sole purpose is to be prepared to "conduct prompt and sustained combat operations at sea."

While the term "up or out" has a somewhat ruthless tone to it, the navy's promotion system is in fact very fair. It ensures that everyone has an equal opportunity for promotion, and it provides fair, clear, and frequent indicators of progress. For the enlisted personnel, a system of detailed written tests are used, along with a weighted multiple that incorporates years in service, test score, awards, and other analytic factors, to determine who will be advanced every six months.

For chief petty officers and officers, selection boards are convened by the secretary of the navy, records are thoroughly reviewed, and individuals are selected for promotion strictly on the merits of their careers. A selection board is a group of individuals senior to those being considered for promotion and who are bound by law to conduct a fair and honest evaluation of the written records before them and to make decisions concerning promotion. The process is scrupulously protected by law, closely supervised by the entire navy leadership, and eminently fair to the individuals being judged.

As a navy spouse, you will hear a great deal of discussion from your sailor and friends about the entire promotion system. There will be endless talks of test scores and opportunity for advancement in a given exam cycle at the enlisted level. The same discussions will go on within the chief's mess and the officer's wardroom, with individuals examining upcoming promotion boards and trying to determine how they will turn out. Your role is the same as any spouse's: be a good listener, try to encourage your sailor to do his or her absolute best in every situation, and recognize that the navy is a very competitive (and fair) playing field, with promotions going to the most deserving.

By most deserving I mean that, as a general rule, promotions will be given to those who study hard for exams (E-6 and below); win awards by working hard at their jobs; complete their professional qualifications (enlisted surface warfare, aviation aircrew, submarine dolphins); maintain a sharp, military appearance through physical fitness and proper wearing of the uniform; and take demanding jobs both at sea and ashore. Sea duty always helps promotion opportunity, whereas staying ashore for an extended period will not help your sailor to advance, whether enlisted or officer. You should know that weight problems will make promotion more difficult, because a CO cannot promote or even recommend for promotion those who fail to meet physical readiness standards.

While your sailor should certainly be aware of the promotion system and actively and contentiously seek promotion, neither of you should obsess over it. Sometimes an expected promotion will not materialize for a variety of reasons. Don't let your sailor get discouraged or bitter. Your spouse's hard work, best efforts, and communication with his or her chain of command will eventually win promotion on merit. A good sailor does not work for the promotion, but rather seeks always to do a good job. The chain of command will then take care of the promotion process.

Basic Medical Care

Being married to a sailor means that you and your immediate family will be provided basic health care throughout his or her active duty enlistment or service. If your sailor proceeds to retirement status (i.e., remains in for twenty or more years), your benefits will continue throughout your life and your spouse's; your children will be covered until they pass the age of twenty-one (or meet certain other guidelines noted below). There are approximately eight million people with access to the military health care system.

Your spouse will obtain complete medical and dental care for no charge. For you and your children, as well as any other full-time dependents (parents who live with you and are completely dependent on you), the system becomes more complicated.

The first step is to enroll in the DoD's medical program, the Defense Enrollment Eligibility Reporting System, or DEERS. You do this by filling out a simple form obtained by your sailor from the personnel office on the ship or shore station. Everyone who is eligible must be enrolled. If you are unsure as to whether you and the entire family are enrolled, call the DEERS Beneficiary Telephone Center at 1-800-538-9552.

Eligibility is as follows:

you and any children under twenty-one, including adopted children or those in legal custody

children older than twenty-one who are or have become severely handicapped and who are dependent on you for at least half their support

unmarried children up to twenty-three years old who are in college

parents or parents-in-law receiving at least half their support from you

widows and widowers who have not remarried

There are some complicated exceptions to the above conditions specific to "former spouses" (i.e., divorced spouses). If you are a divorced spouse and are unclear as to your legal claim to medical care, check with your nearest military hospital's patient affairs office. In general, you must have been married for at least twenty years during your former sailor's service, including fifteen years of active duty.

The means of providing medical care can vary widely depending on where you are stationed. If you are in the vicinity of a large navy hospital (Balboa in San Diego, Portsmouth in Norfolk, or Bethesda in Washington, D.C., for example), you may be able to obtain both inpatient and outpatient care directly from the military, essentially as your sailor does. If you are in an area without a large navy medical component, you may need to obtain medical treatment "on the economy," using the new TRICARE system. This is described in chapter 3, under "Advanced Medical and Dental Care."

In general, obtaining direct care from the navy is reasonably convenient and is the least expensive method of securing treatment. The quality varies widely, however, and it can be frustrating at times due to overloaded facilities. Going "on the economy" via the TRICARE system offers you a series of options, although it does include a growing component of self-financing. You can also do a combination of sorts, signing up for an appropriate TRICARE program while still obtaining some direct care. Direct care can come from what are called PRIMUS or NavCare clinics, which are established in civilian centers with large military populations, and which provide day-to-day care. They are staffed with civilian doctors, but the quality of care can be uneven—due to the wide variation in physician quality and overcrowding at the facilities. These clinics can be useful for extremely minor problems, however—the "run of the mill" bad colds, flu bugs, ear infections—and for filling basic prescriptions.

Basic Dental Care

Your sailor is entitled to full dental care provided directly through the command. Occasionally, the navy dental clinic has room to provide some dental care to spouses and children, although this is definitely *not* something you should count on. The best course of action is to enroll your family in the TRICARE active duty family members' dental plan, United Concordia, which is, in effect, an inexpensive and limited dental insurance offered to the military through the DoD. It covers treatment by civilian dentists and is quite cost effective: less than ten dollars per month for one family member, and about twenty dollars per month total for more than one family member. For a "typical" family of three dependents, that is roughly eighty dollars per year for each member—

far less than the cost of the two semiannual check-ups and cleanings per year, and 80 percent of most basic related work (fillings). Concordia will cover 50 percent of more complicated work (root canals, dentures, removals), and will make a single payment of $1,200 toward braces.

I advise you to encourage your sailor to enroll in this dental plan, because trying to pay independently for even a simple cleaning plus a filling or two can be very costly. Concordia is a cost-effective preventive plan that may even encourage you to visit the dentist for regular checkups.

Some Observations on Navy Medical Care

As an active-duty navy spouse, you probably will be fairly comfortable with the routine medical coverage provided by the navy. While you may from time to time meet a few "contract" physicians (i.e., civilians hired on a contractual basis) who don't impress you, overall navy medical care is quite good, if somewhat industrial in its approach. Generally, the uniformed physicians are excellent, motivated, and very caring. The odds are good that all you need in the way of routine treatment will be available at either a local navy hospital or clinic, or a even a basic PRIMUS/ NavCare clinic.

As we will discuss in chapter 3, you will need to make a decision on the type of TRICARE protection you desire, then a secondary decision on whether to add a supplemental insurance policy. If you are a healthy family, particularly if you are generally stationed in areas with large and readily available navy medical facilities, you probably will not require additional insurance. On the other hand, if you have a family member with current or potentially serious medical problems, you would be well advised to take the highest level of TRICARE coverage and add a supplemental insurance policy.

You also should be aware of navy assistance in less likely areas of medical concern such as substance abuse, mental health, AIDS, and extended family illness. If you or someone in your family has a problem with alcohol or other drugs, there is support and some treatment available through either the local NFSC or the navy medical facilities. Many individual commands have drug and alcohol program advisors (DAPAs) with information on these programs. Smoking cessation information is also generally available from the same sources. Mental health is treated through the local navy medical system, as is AIDS. If you are faced with the extended illness of a family member, you may be eligible for a stay in a Fisher House. These privately funded lodgings are located near military and Veterans Administration (VA) hospitals, including navy hospitals in Bethesda (Washington, D.C.), Portsmouth (Norfolk), and San Diego. The cost of a stay is nominal, generally about ten dollars each night.

Conclusion

While there will be many challenges ahead, I think you will find that the normal day-to-day life of a navy spouse is a fun and wonderful experience. In the next chapter, we will discuss what to do when storms are sighted out ahead of your track.

3
Smooth Sailing

Oh to go down to the sea again, to the lovely sea and the sky,
And all I ask is a tall ship, and a star to steer her by.

"Sea-Fever"
John Masefield

Once you are reasonably settled into the routine of navy life, you will gradually find that things seem easier, and your course will settle smoothly into a relatively normal path. But just as your spouse uses navigational aids at sea to find the right course to sail and thus avoid troublesome rocks, weather, and shoals, you will need to attend to a few routine items as you sail along in your navy life. In this chapter you will find a few ideas for dealing with the day-to-day business unique to navy life.

Navy Family Service Centers (NFSC)

One of the most important places on your nearby naval base is the Navy Family Service Center. This organization is staffed by helpful counselors who specialize in providing assistance to navy family members. Their primary product is information, and they offer classes, seminars, phone-in advice, pamphlets, maps, packages, and publications that cover virtually every aspect of navy life. They also offer relocation assistance, including hospitality kits (cooking and eating utensils, roll-away beds, irons, high chairs); libraries packed with regional resources; a spouse employment assistance program for finding you a job in a new area; and many education and counseling programs. The NFSC can be a gold mine for any navy family if used to its full extent.

Thus one of the first stops for any navy spouse should be the closest NFSC, and a good way to learn about their services is to attend one of their "Welcome Aboard" seminars. Normally about two hours, these sessions will provide an abundance of excellent information. More important, a visit will provide you with a face-to-face introduction to the helpful people at the NFSC. Throughout this book, you will find references to the NFSC; in chapter 4 we will discuss in more detail how to use them. The sooner you make a trip to *your* center, the happier you will be.

Personal Affairs

The first and best thing you can do is *get organized*. Navy life is complicated enough without the additional confusion of disorganization to plague you, so begin to organize your personal affairs by first buying a small file cabinet. You don't need anything elaborate or expensive; in fact, a cardboard box will do the trick temporarily. Once the box has served its purpose, however, I recommend that you purchase a metal cabinet large enough initially to hold about twenty file jackets. As you move through navy life, you may find you need a larger cabinet; the point is to start with something to keep important papers in one location.

Use the following headings for your personal affairs files: ID Cards, Power of Attorney, Wills, Direct Deposit and Allotments, Medical, Dental, Insurance, Leave and Earnings Statements, and Helpful Contacts.

ID Cards

Your ID card is the first thing you should obtain after marrying a sailor. This card is your "ticket" to many of the benefits of being a navy spouse, and it is also nearly universally accepted in the civilian sector as guaranteed identification for cashing a check, obtaining a driver's license or registration, verifying your age, and so forth. Within the navy establishment, you will need your ID card for entering the exchange or commissary, going to any military facility (base theater, gardening shop, gasoline station, child care center), or obtaining medical care. Today's ID cards have bar codes and are quite durable, and they include a photograph; height, weight, and age information; and the identity of the issuing command. Besides you and your spouse, children ten years or older also should have an ID card. Children retain their ID cards until they leave the household permanently or reach the age of twenty-three. Spouses and children of retired navy personnel also retain ID cards.

Obtaining your ID card is relatively simple, and the entire process should take you less than an hour. The first step is to have your sailor fill out a form at the command that certifies you as an official spouse. To do this, the sailor will need a copy of the marriage certificate for you, and birth certificates for any children. The form, a DD398, is very easy to complete, and will be signed by the personnel officer at your spouse's command.

Once you have this form, go to the Personnel Support Activity (PSA) or Personnel Support Detachment (PSD) on the closest navy base. If you

are not near a navy base, have your spouse verify the correct location—
it may be a nearby army base, for example. And sometimes your spouse's
command can actually issue the ID card themselves. If you do go to a
PSA or PSD, you will find it is normally somewhere near the headquarters building. If you are unsure about the location, have your spouse
check at his or her command, or ask the guard at the gate. Inside the
PSA/PSD, there will be a small special section where ID cards are issued.
You normally sign in at the front desk and wait briefly while the petty
officer types up the card. Your picture will then be taken (so remember
to look your best, since you will live with the photo for five years) and
affixed to the ID card. Finally, it will be laminated and presented to you.

Be careful with your ID card. There is a black market that resells
stolen and lost ID cards, and they can be used in several fraudulent
ways. If you do lose it, report its loss at once. Your sailor will have to
explain the circumstances, usually in writing, and reapply for a new one.
Children in particular should be cautioned to be very careful with their
ID cards. You may find it is best to retain their ID cards until they are
old enough to be responsible for them.

In your ID card file, keep a copy of the documents you used to obtain
your card, as well as a copy of the front of your card (in case it is lost or
stolen).

Power of Attorney

Something you will certainly become familiar with during your spouse's
time in the navy is a power of attorney. This is a legal term, and it permits you to take action on your spouse's behalf while he or she is at sea
or on a forward deployment. There are several variations of the power
of attorney, and they range from the *general* power of attorney, which
means you have complete authority to sign *anything* on your spouse's
behalf; to *special* powers of attorney, which are very specific, for discrete
tasks such as buying a house or applying for a car loan.

Which power of attorney to obtain is something you and your spouse
need to discuss. You should look at factors such as the length of your
marriage, the duration of the upcoming separation, what legal activities
you will need to undertake on your spouse's behalf, and the complexity
of your affairs. In general, if you have a fairly simple legal situation and
are not planning on any major purchases (such as a house or car), you
may want to execute a limited power of attorney. If you have a more
complicated situation (several children, a pending move, a car purchase), you may want to execute a general power of attorney.

Obtaining a power of attorney is fairly simple and will not cost you
anything. Your command will probably arrange for a navy lawyer to

visit during the months leading up to a deployment, and will make counseling available to help you decide what type of power of attorney to execute. If the command does not have an active program in this regard, you can simply make an appointment at the Navy Legal Service Office (NLSO), and they will provide the service. The NLSO is sometimes referred to as, simply, "base legal."

In general, if your sailor is headed out to sea for longer than thirty days, it is a good idea to have at least a limited power of attorney on hand, and if a longer cruise is coming up and there are complex issues pending, a general power of attorney should be considered. Don't find yourself unprepared for any unforeseen situations that may come up.

Wills

Some people are averse to executing a will, but it is a simple document that can make life a great deal easier for survivors in the event of your spouse's death, and everyone in the armed services should have one drawn up. The navy provides resources to do so at no expense, and it is a relatively simple process.

The first stop is your spouse's command, because many ships, squadrons, and shore installations have an annual "legal focus" day in which legal counseling and the opportunity to execute wills and powers of attorney are readily available. Many deploying units such as ships, submarines, and aircraft squadrons work hard to ensure that everyone in the crew has a will executed before a full 180-day deployment. The process involves bringing a navy lawyer to the installation for a day, during which time the rough wills are drawn up, then having the lawyer return in a week for the signing of the wills.

If the command does not provide such a service, go to the NLSO. You can call and make an appointment to see a lawyer, who will then guide you through the process free of charge. After the will is prepared, you must return to the office to sign it.

Once you have executed your will, keep it in your file cabinet and provide someone close to you—parents or close friends—with a copy as well.

Direct Deposit

One of the quickest ways to organize your finances is to set up a direct deposit system for your sailor's pay. This means that the money, instead of being paid out to the individual, will be electronically deposited into your bank account on the 1st and 15th of each month. The funds then will be immediately available to draw checks on, withdraw with your

ATM card, or accrue interest. Most commands today strongly encourage their sailors to execute direct deposit systems, and it makes life much simpler on payday. Another advantage is that, once established, it will not change until you direct it otherwise, so when you transfer, your account goes with you. To keep things simple, you may want to consider a financial institution with branches in most navy locations. A good choice is the Navy Federal Credit Union, which has an excellent reputation for good service and many convenient locations for navy people.

Once you have selected direct deposit, your spouse's entire paycheck, minus any money you have chosen to place elsewhere through an allotment, will be available on payday. Normally you will receive a small, printed piece of paper from your sailor's command indicating the exact amount of money deposited into the account. If for some reason you do not receive this information promptly, there are two things you should do. First, have your spouse see the command's disbursing officer to ensure that the office has the correct mailing address. Second, call the designated financial institution (most will have an 800 number) and verify the last deposit (and its exact amount) made to the account.

Another helpful feature of direct deposit is that you can split the paycheck. You can do this at the financial institution by ordering the money placed in two separate accounts (very helpful if your sailor is under way a great deal), or through the navy, with the sailor receiving a portion of his or her pay at the command. Again, this is very helpful when your sailor is assigned to sea duty and under way a great deal—it will make balancing the checkbook far easier.

Allotments

Allotments are somewhat like direct deposit. They permit you to allocate a specific amount of your spouse's pay for a defined purpose. Examples include placing a set amount of money in an account, fund, or investment; buying U.S. savings bonds; paying rent to a landlord's account directly; or sending money to a charity. Allotments are an excellent means of setting up a simple investment program. Amounts as small as fifty dollars per month can be set up for a mutual fund or savings bonds. The advantage of an allotment is that you never see the money, because it goes directly into the investment—you cannot spend what you don't see in your account each month. Believe me, it is a good idea to "pay yourself first" on payday by automatically putting some percentage of your spouse's paycheck (try for 5 to 10 percent) into an investment program through an allotment.

There are several different kinds of allotments, including the following:

"D" Dependent—sent to the spouse at home

"B" Bond—immediately buys a government savings bond, which is sent to a directed address

"C" Charity—contributes to a charity, normally government- or navy-sponsored drives such as the Navy–Marine Corps Relief Society (NMCRS) or the Combined Federal Campaign (CFC)

"H" Home Mortgage

"I" Insurance

"L" Loan

"S" Savings

Some things to remember about allotments: they go into effect or are canceled on the first payday of the month following execution of the allotment, so they are not instantaneous; they are free to execute, no matter how many you have or how often you need to change them; and they must be established with the disbursing office at your spouse's command. As a general rule, start an allotment at least three months prior to the start of the requirement (loan, mortgage, dependent, etc.). This will give time for the system to smooth itself out.

Family Finances during Deployment

To provide for the family while deployed, your sailor's best option is direct deposit into the family checking account, with the sailor receiving a portion via a split payment. Or you could take out a "D" allotment for the amount you will need on the home front, with the remainder going to the sailor via the command. If you choose the latter, *make sure your sailor starts the allotment early and does not change it.* The command will know when your sailor is deploying for more than a month overseas, and an advance payment can be set up so that the allotment is, in effect, paid "up front," without your waiting for the normal deduction-followed-by-payment sequence. The advance pay will be deducted over a period of up to six months—essentially an interest-free loan from the navy to families facing a deployment.

Deployments can be expensive, and you and your spouse should sit down and create a reasonable budget that allocates money fairly between you on the home front and your spouse on deployment. A great deal depends on the number of liberty ports and the spending habits of your sailor. Give careful thought to the distribution of money and mutually discuss your plans for staying within your agreed budgets. Home front costs to support the family will remain fairly constant, despite the departure of your sailor. Nevertheless, your sailor needs money in his or her pocket to take advantage of those precious liberty port days.

One way families get into trouble is through credit cards and telephone charges. If your sailor uses a credit card freely in foreign ports, but the bills come to you, you are asking for trouble. The same applies to telephone bills. Self-discipline is the answer, as is putting your sailor on a pure cash basis. Encourage your spouse to maintain the budget, or severe problems can emerge.

Pay Problems

If you encounter a pay problem, the first stop is always the command's disbursing office, where your sailor's pay record is monitored (although all master pay records are electronically maintained in Cleveland, Ohio, at the Naval Finances Center). If your command does not have its own disbursing office, your sailor should check with the PSD on the base; or you can call the DoD Finance Center at 1-800-346-3374. If, while your sailor is deployed, you have a problem that cannot be resolved by contacting him or her, discuss it with the command ombudsman (see chapter 4) or a counselor at the NFSC. If there is a pay emergency, contact the NMRCS or the American Red Cross (see chapter 4) for additional help.

Basic Finance

As you set up your basic personal affairs, you should establish a simple and effective finance plan. While a detailed discussion of family finances is beyond the scope of this book, there are excellent resources available to you—at no cost—through the navy that will help you set up a financial plan for your navy family.

The first stop is the NFSC, where various publications and seminars are offered that will help you organize your finances. Additionally, the public library offers simple how-to books on arranging your family finances. The basics of any financial plan are quite simple.

First, make sure you know exactly how much money you have coming *into* the family. This is a matter of simply checking the LES that your sailor receives each month from the command. Add to your navy salary any money earned from *your* job, as well as any additional part-time income, interest on investments, or regular sources of funds you may be receiving. Worksheets that will show you how to categorize your pay are available from the NFSC.

Next, you need to determine how much money you *spend* in an average month. This may take several months to determine, and you must keep track of everything you spend. Using the worksheets from the NFSC will help you determine your expenses, and you may be surprised at how much you spend on incidentals without really noticing it—until you write it all down. Watch, for example, the costs of incidentals at work over the course of a month—a daily newspaper, cup of coffee, bagel, or even a daily lunch—can add up over a month and generally are avoidable. "Brown-bagging it" is often a real money-saver. These sorts of things will become apparent quickly if you carefully track what you spend each month.

Another key focus in your budget is *credit*. While taking advantage of credit can be essential in certain situations (buying a house or car, for example), it can be a trap. A real danger is the use of credit cards, which charge high rates of interest, to buy day-to-day goods that are outside the budget—stereos, expensive or unnecessary clothes, vacations, or entertainment. Once faced with credit bills bearing high interest rates, the navy family can find it very difficult to return to a solid financial situation, where everything is paid off each month and at least 5 percent of your total income is being put aside as savings.

This is a situation where financial counseling can be helpful. Once you have calculated your income and expenses and have a clear picture of your credit and debt, go to the NFSC and take one of their financial seminars (offered monthly, quarterly, and annually, depending on the subject and demand). They cover everything from setting up a basic financial plan to breaking the debt cycle. Another good resource that should be available through your command is personal financial management (PFM), which will normally include access to trained volunteer financial counselors. Have your sailor inquire at work as to whether or not your command has a PFM program in place. The NFSC and PFM offer help in money management strategies, understanding pay and allowances, credit management, savings and investments, car buying, and consumer rip-offs.

Other ways to avoid credit problems include not using credit cards at all, or keeping only one for emergency purposes. And if you don't need anything, stay out of stores—shopping for entertainment leads to unnecessary bills. Try to curb impulse purchases—this applies to your sailor overseas as well. Before deployment, be sure to have a frank discussion with him or her about the extent to which credit cards will be used (if at all). The beautiful Tabriz oriental rug from Bahrain, charged on credit, may not look so beautiful when it comes time to pay the bill at home. The bottom line: budget yourself—you can do it.

When you start putting a little bit away every month (even if it's only fifty to a hundred dollars), you will be amazed at how quickly it will grow into a significant nest egg. Do this by taking out an allotment to a conservative mutual fund or by starting a savings bond program. Your command financial specialist or the counselor at the NFSC can advise

Money Stealers

There are many things in life that don't seem very expensive on the spur of the moment, from a $2.19 cappuccino at Starbucks to a $35.00 per month membership at a health club. But if you were to figure how much they cost in the course of a year, you might be very surprised. Remember that a little savings each month—as little as a hundred dollars or so placed in a basic mutual fund or used to buy a U.S. savings bond—will add up to a considerable amount twenty years from now, while the benefits of the health club (which you seldom get to anyway) can be found for free by walking through the neighborhood or working out at the navy gym.

This does not mean you should deny yourself a few videos on a Friday night, but do be careful that some of the following "money stealers" don't take a bigger dent out of your wallet than you intend:

aerobic clubs	child lunches	lunches
alimony	cigarettes	magazines
baby pictures	club dues	music lessons
baby-sitting	cosmetics	newspapers
bank charges	diaper service	pets
beauty parlor	domestic help	postage
beer	dry-cleaning	race fees
bikes	encyclopedias	skating
bottled water	entertainment	sodas
bowling	garden	sports
burgers	gifts	stamps
cable TV/movie	greeting cards	stationery
channels	gyms	tapes
car washes	hobbies	toys
card games	jazzercise	videos
charity contributions	late charges	wine
child allowances	laundry	
child associations	lottery	

you as to the advantages of each, but the key is to *start early in your life and save with regularity.* Don't buy into a "get rich quick" scheme. You should make regular payments, consider an individual retirement account (IRA) due to the tax advantages, and use an allotment system to put money directly into savings before you even see it. Savings can make all the difference in emergency situations and when you look toward retirement and life after the navy. You will be glad you planned ahead.

Bill Collectors

If you find yourself with credit problems, you may receive calls and notices from bill collectors. You should be aware of the Fair Debt Collection Practices Act, which gives you rights as a debtor: Bill collectors cannot threaten you in any way, use obscene or profane language, make annoying or harassing telephone calls, imply they are working for a government agency (i.e., the Internal Revenue Service or a police department), or ridicule you.

If you feel that a bill collector is hounding you unnecessarily or illegally, contact your sailor's command (through the ombudsman), the NLSO, or the NFSC for help. Of course, you should make every effort to meet your legally incurred obligations and work with your creditors to find a mutually satisfactory solution to your credit problems. The key, as always, is to ask for help if you find yourself overwhelmed. Creditors are generally willing to work out alternative payment plans for you rather than have you try to walk away from the problem. Face up to any early bad decisions you have made, ask for help in organizing your finances, and things will work out.

Insurance

There are several key types of insurance, and your personal affairs folder on this important topic should be subdivided into three main sections: Automobile, Life, and Home/Property.

Automobile insurance is required in virtually every state in the country and is widely available. In deciding which company to select, a good source is *Consumer Reports* magazine. Every few years they rate all insurance companies in the United States based on financial stability, customer satisfaction, responsiveness during crises, timeliness of claim payment, and so forth. The most recent report should be available in your local library. One highly recommended company that works frequently with the military is United Services Automobile Association (USAA)—but there are other fine companies as well. Shop around and consult the references.

In terms of life insurance, you should be aware that the military provides a basic package on your sailor. Called the Serviceman's Group Life Insurance (SGLI), it automatically provides $100,000 to designated survivors in the event of the member's death. For a very small fee, your sailor can increase this coverage to $250,000, making it a sound financial investment. [Coverage is available for spouse and children, too.] If your family is small (just the two of you, or a single young child), this may be sufficient, particularly if you work. If you are further along in your career, have more children and a mortgage on a house, or you are at home raising the children, taking additional simple term life insurance, perhaps another $100,000 to $200,000, is advisable. *Consumer Reports* is also a good resource in this area, and it can be easily found at the library. Most financial planners advocate simple term insurance (rather than more elaborate policies that combine insurance and savings programs together) for young, healthy families.

Home and property insurance is a category of coverage that varies widely depending on your particular situation. If you own your own home, you normally will be legally required by your mortgage company to have insurance sufficient to cover the house itself. You should investigate taking out additional property insurance to cover yourself in the event of catastrophic loss (fire, flood). Normally this is not very expensive, and it provides a good financial umbrella. Generally, the longer you have been married and the more goods you have accumulated, the more important this becomes. Again, check with *Consumer Reports* for ideas on the best companies in this area.

Keep all of your policies together in your personal affairs files, and review them at least once a year—perhaps as part of your annual income tax preparation. Both you and your spouse should be up-to-speed on your coverage in all areas. Tax time is a wise moment to do this, as you will be working with your entire financial portfolio at once.

Finally, bear in mind that insurance sales representatives generally work on commission and have a vested interest in one company's policies. Be careful of overly aggressive salespersons who may try to direct you into policies and insurance you may not need. It is better to talk to an independent financial advisor who does not deal in insurance sales about the amount of insurance you need. Your command financial specialist can give you initial guidance.

Advance Financial Planning and Resources

As you move further along in your navy career, you will see greater financial rewards. Although your spouse's navy salary will never make you rich, the navy offers a solid level of income to those who do well, work hard, and advance through the ranks. While those just starting out may find this difficult to believe, as time goes by, you will find both the need and the resources to make larger investment decisions about savings and investments.

When you are just starting out, the key is to consolidate your income, ensure you live within your budget, avoid the credit trap, and *start a small but steady savings program*. At about the five-year point, as your spouse (I hope) decides to make the navy a career, you should sit down with a financial planner and try to map out a strategy for what might be called your "5–10–20 Plan" (referring to the next five, ten, and twenty years). This plan should focus on your long-term goals, which may include saving for your children's college educations, buying and ultimately paying off your own home, and establishing an IRA to supplement your navy retirement and, ultimately, your social security funds in your golden years.

Naturally, a great deal can—and will—change in your life over the next twenty years. You may move very smoothly through promotion and advances in income, avoid any surprise expenses, and attain a twenty-year retirement, or remain in the navy longer. On the other hand, you may face unexpected events ranging from divorce, to illness, to a windfall inheritance. You cannot plan for every potential unexpected event, but you can build a structure that allows you to respond well to changes that *do* emerge.

Your 5–10–20 Plan should include not only your long-range goals, but where you think you will find yourself at each of the points along the path to financial security. While this level of planning is beyond that normally offered by a command financial specialist or the NFSC, they can give you ideas and resources for setting up a longer-range plan. Do some preliminary research in the library, reading financial magazines (*Money, Consumer Reports, Investor*) and books. Then see a chartered financial analyst who can help you set up an investment program. Your command financial specialist should be able to provide several recommendations for advanced advisors in your sailor's immediate area.

Helpful Contacts

Your personal affairs file should also contain a folder of helpful contacts. Many of these are discussed in depth in chapter 4, and they range from your NFSC to the command ombudsman. You will also want to keep in one place the numbers of all of your insurance companies, credit card companies, and other organizations with which you do business. This list can be particularly helpful if you lose your wallet and need to cancel credit cards (do so immediately) or reconstruct your documents. The contact folder should also have the emergency numbers of family and friends, as well as the local navy hospital or clinic. And the NFSC should be able to provide you with a list of telephone numbers and contacts for your region. Many commands provide a small, wallet-sized card with emergency numbers printed on it. Have your sailor check on the availability of such a card with the command master chief.

Advanced Medical and Dental Care

Medical

In the last chapter we discussed the basics of obtaining medical care and your rights and responsibilities as a navy spouse. This section will

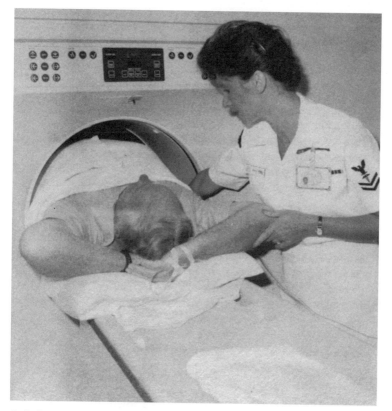

Medical care at a naval hospital. U.S. Naval Institute collection.

discuss some of the more complicated issues surrounding medical and dental care, which have been changing dramatically over the past five years, reflecting the larger, ongoing national debate over health care. Recognize that this is one of the most flexible areas of navy information, so double-check information here with appropriate sources. As always, your command ombudsman and the NFSC are good starting points to direct you on medical and dental care, although they will probably pass you directly to your health benefits advisors (HBAs; sometimes called the TRICARE office) at the closest navy hospital or clinic for information.

The overall military health care system is moving into a new approach called TRICARE—a health care program for all active-duty and retired military personnel and their dependents. Over the next few years, TRICARE will be fully examined as it overcomes start-up challenges, and time will tell if this system is the solution to many of the problems navy spouses have faced in dealing with medical challenges.

TRICARE is a nationwide system that provides beneficiaries with three options:

• TRICARE Prime: Similar to civilian health maintenance organizations (HMOs), this provides better and more personalized service to the military health care consumer than in the past. All active-duty members will be enrolled in Prime and will continue to receive most of their care from military medical personnel. Family members are eligible to enroll in Prime and will then have a military or civilian primary care manager (PCM), whom you should think of as a family physician or pediatrician for nonemergency, routine health care. Cost shares for Prime are the least expensive of the three options.

• TRICARE Extra: This option allows you to choose your own care providers. Assuming you use an authorized network provider (i.e., a physician who agrees to standard fees), a 5 percent discount from TRICARE Standard cost shares is available. A standard annual deductible of $150 for individuals and $300 per family must be met before the system will begin cost sharing. Once the deductible is met, TRICARE will pay 85 percent of the fee for the physician you select, and all but about ten dollars per day for inpatient care. The advantage here is that you can select the doctor you want, but you will pay a bit more for the care you obtain.

• TRICARE Standard: This was formerly known as CHAMPUS, and it essentially amounts to declining to enroll in TRICARE and continuing to pay CHAMPUS costs. This sounds complicated, but it isn't. This option affords the consumer an unlimited choice of providers, but it is the most expensive way to go. You will still have to meet the $150 individual/$300 family deductible, then you will be responsible for 20 percent of the allowable charges. Remember that 20 percent of an expensive procedure can be a great deal of money, although there are so-called "catastrophic caps" in place that limit ultimate cost to $1,000 for active-duty members and $7,500 for retirees.

These three options are summarized in table 3.1.

These options can be discussed in depth with your HBA to determine which program is best for you. If you are a young and healthy navy family with a limited need for health care, the best system probably would be TRICARE Prime, which is virtually free, particularly for E1 through E4 families. If selecting your physician is important to you, perhaps because of medical challenges in your family, either TRICARE Extra or TRICARE Standard may be a better choice. There are no enrollment fees for active-duty families. Retiree families will have higher costs and somewhat reduced benefits.

Dental

For many years, there was no dental coverage for military spouses and dependents in the continental United States, although the military

Table 3.1. What will TRICARE Cost?

	TRICARE Prime E1–E4	TRICARE Prime E5 and above	TRICARE Extra	TRICARE Standard
Annual deductible	$0	$0	$150 individual, $300 family, $50/$100 for E4 & below	
Civilian outpatient visit	$6	$12	15% of negotiated fee	20% of allowable charge
Civilian inpatient admission	$11 per day ($25 minimum)	$11 per day ($25 minimum)	Greater of $25 or $10.45 per day	Greater of $25 or $10.45 per day
Civilian inpatient mental health	$20 per day	$20 per day	$20 per day	$20 per day

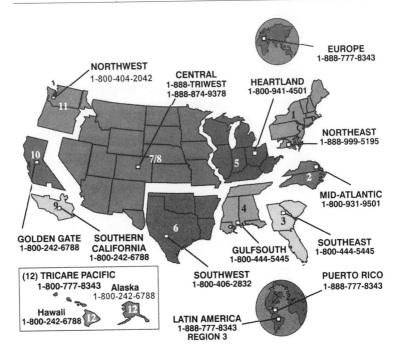

provided free dental care for active-duty personnel. Over the past decade, a new program that provides dental insurance for spouses and dependents has been created, and your spouse can elect to take advantage of it through his or her command.

The insurance, known as United Concordia, provides dental care to families of members stationed in the continental United States, Guam, Puerto Rico, and the U.S. Virgin Islands. (In many overseas locations, dental work is provided by the military to spouses and dependents.) It is currently run by the United Concordia Companies of Camp Hill, Pennsylvania. Membership is not automatic, so your spouse should enroll at the command by completing form DD2494. Once you are enrolled, you must remain with the program for a minimum of two years. The cost is quite minimal, roughly twenty dollars per month for the family, and it covers most routine preventive dental work (checkups, fluoride treatment). It will also cover a percentage of dental repair work (e.g., 80 percent for fillings, up to $1,000 annually). It also provides up to $1,200 for orthodontic work over the life of a given patient. This is a good basic dental plan, and if you are not covered where you work, this is the best way to go through the navy.

Additional Medical Information

Before you can receive any care, you must be enrolled in DEERS. To check the status of a member of your family, you can call DEERS directly at 1-800-538-9552. Your local navy medical center can also check this quickly for you on the telephone.

The web site for TRICARE is <http://www.tricare.osd.mil>. This site covers a wide range of issues you may encounter and also includes up-to-date contact information for the various TRICARE regional offices, each of which has its own web site. Some of the major regional telephone numbers are:

Region 1 Northeast (National Capital): (888) 999-5195
Region 2 Mid-Atlantic (Portsmouth): (800) 931-9501
Region 3 Southeast (Eisenhower): (800) 444-5445
Region 9 Southern California (San Diego): (800) 242-6788
Region 12 Hawaii and Alaska: (800) 242-6788
TRICARE Pacific: (888) 777-8343
TRICARE Europe: (888) 777-8343

The web site for the elective (but highly recommended) navy dental plan, underwritten by United Concordia, is <http://www. ucci.com>.

Fisher House

If you find yourself dealing with a seriously ill family member who is undergoing a prolonged hospital stay, you should be aware of the opportunity to stay at a Fisher House. The houses are privately funded lodgings that are supported through the Combined Federal Campaign. They are named for Zachary and Elizabeth Fisher, the civilian couple who established them so that military families would have a low-cost housing alternative when a family member is hospitalized. There are currently twenty-eight Fisher houses, with three more currently under construction. Many Fisher houses are located at or near major navy hospitals, including Balboa in California, Portsmouth in Virginia, and Bethesda in Maryland. They can accommodate an entire family in nice sized suites and the cost is minimal (about $10 per night), with several free. Visit their web site at <http:www.fisherhouse.org>. You can also contact them through their toll-free number (888-294-8560) or their email address (*FisherHouse@aol.com*).

Legal Issues

Ideally, you will not find yourself involved in any complex legal affairs, but if you do, be aware that the navy offers some assistance in this area.

Your navy legal assistance program can provide help from the Judge Advocate Generals (navy lawyers, or "JAGs") regarding personal legal rights and responsibilities.

A JAG is a law school graduate and is licensed by the federal court. He or she is also a graduate of the Naval Justice School in Newport, Rhode Island. JAGs work in the NLSOs found at all navy bases. They can write up wills; provide powers of attorney and bills of sale; assist with domestic relations issues such as adoptions, separations, or nonsupport cases; provide referrals to civilian lawyers for divorces; notarize or depose; assist on contracts, leases, and tax questions; help with consumer problems; and counsel you on citizenship, immigration, and passport issues.

They do not provide defense assistance in civilian criminal cases, but they will provide help to service members in courts-martial, reenlistment disputes, or other problems related directly to your spouse's service. All conversations and dealings with spouses are in strict confidence and are protected by a military version of the lawyer-client privilege laws.

Predeployment Thoughts

We will discuss some of the personal challenges associated with deployments in more detail later, but this is a good time to cover quickly some of the practical issues that come up before a cruise. Any time your sailor is away for more than two or three weeks—and certainly before any standard 180-day deployment—you both should take a quick look at legal, financial, and other practical matters. Use your filing system to cover everything from health care to life insurance, and make sure you have thought through the issues. You can obtain a very handy predeployment checklist from the NFSC, but here are a few points to consider:

- Legal residence: make sure your records will be sent to the right address, that you both have absentee ballot information, and that emergency data information is updated at home and at the command.

- Power of attorney: consult with the NLSO on the need for and the specific drafting of a power of attorney.

- Personal affairs: go through your files and clear them out, make sure ID cards are current, and conclude any personal legal business requiring you and your spouse's presence.

- Finances: create a budget, carefully covering who will spend what at home and at the deployment command. Ensure that you have thought through how money will get to both of you. Limit credit card use to true emergencies. Make sure that sending your sailor on a long cruise does not create new problems.

• Wills: read and update your own and your sailor's wills. Investigate the possibility of a living will, which describes your wishes in the event you or your sailor are incapacitated due to medical problems. Make sure there are several witnessed copies in different locations, accessible to parents or other trusted friends.

• Personal property: arrange care and storage for belongings, pets, and vehicles as necessary. Inventory household goods, making a video if possible. Store these in a safe location away from the home.

• Life insurance: review your life insurance situation, ensuring SGLI is maximized (done at the command by your sailor). Ensure sufficient coverage on both you and your sailor, and that in your sailor's case it does not have an exemption for death in a war or in combat. This is extremely unlikely, but it's worth checking.

• Medical and dental coverage: ensure that your DEERS registration is up to date, that your dental plan is in effect, and that you have everything you need to tap the medical system while your spouse is deployed.

Taking Care of Your Navy Children

Naturally, one of the most important aspects of smooth sailing in the navy sphere is making sure your children are well situated. At the top of working parents' lists is child care. As a result of more spouses entering the work force, the navy has worked very hard to help our families solve the challenges associated with finding quality care. As a result, the Navy Child Development Program currently provides families in all fleet concentration areas with three key resources: resources and referral programs run by the Family Service Centers, child development centers, and child development homes. While the Navy is still struggling to fulfill the needs of many areas, a great deal of progress has been made.

Child Development Centers

The child development centers provide full- and part-time day care in group settings for children under the age of five and are operated by the Department of Defense. Some of the centers offer partial-day preschool as well. They typically are in operation almost twelve hours per day, nominally 6:00 A.M. to 6:00 P.M. on weekdays. The National Academy of

Early Childhood Programs accredits each of the centers and the fees are established by the Department of Defense, based on the total family income. Priority is given to active-duty, single parents or dual-parent families with full-time working/student spouses. All other active-duty, DoD civilian, and retiree families are eligible thereafter.

Child Development Homes

These child development homes are at-home situations set up by a day care provider who is certified by the navy to provide child care for up to six children. This program benefits the navy in two ways. In addition to caring for navy children, the provider is often a navy spouse and creates employment for many families. A child development home often offers extended hours, including weekends and evenings to cover shift work. Generally more flexible than the child development centers, the homes provide a good setting for younger infants and toddlers who require more one-on-one attention. The navy is also working to expand the availability of child care through child development home programs located in off-base certified homes by using parent subsidies and provider incentives. Child development homes may present an opportunity for you to find a good child care situation and also a potential for employment following certification. For additional information, Navy Family Service Centers can provide information for both types of child care as well as full referral information.

LIFELines: A Great Web Site

One of the most exciting new means of gathering information about navy life is through the Department of the Navy's official web site "LIFELines." The site, <http://www.lifelines2000.org>, incorporates five different media (Internet, satellite broadcasting, teleconferencing, cable television, and Internet simulcasting) to provide connectivity with loved ones and a treasure trove of quality-of-life resources. Developed under the direction of Secretary of the Navy Richard Danzig in 1999, the site has been lauded by government officials and Internet communities as a model of how to disperse information to a sizable work force. The site will eventually be integrated with Navy–Marine Corps Intranet, but all the information will remain accessible during the transition. Check with the command ombudsman or the Family Service Center for the current web address if the one provided here does not work.

LIFELines resembles a shopping mall, with its many doors leading to a wide variety of interesting topics. Some of the subjects covered are:

- Commissaries and exchanges (includes locations, hours, and services provided)
- Education (educational benefits, programs, and opportunities)
- Family Support (resources on organizations and services, links, and articles)
- Health care (medical, dental, pharmaceutical resources and information)
- Housing (relocation and housing services such as availability and how to get on a housing list)
- Installation sites (services available on bases in the U.S. and overseas)
- Morale, welfare, and recreation services (links and resources to activities, discounted travel and tickets)
- Transition information (retirement and preretirement separation resources).

In addition you can connect with chaplains, a library, and the business portal, which provides resources on job listings, government employment, consumer information, and personal financial advice. There are links to national and local press web sites so sailors and their spouses can stay connected with their hometowns, and you can usually find recently posted messages from the chief of naval operations, the master chief of the navy, and other senior navy personnel.

As a specific example, you can click on "Relocation and Housing," "Moving the Family," and then "Pets," to find detailed information on moving the family pet overseas. Included are country-by-country standards, vaccination requirements, and other resources for helping you set up the move. You can also check into discussions and question-and-answer sessions on-line and live, as well as post questions and feedback.

LIFELines is a remarkable accomplishment and establishes the Department of the Navy at the forefront in providing electronic information to its large and widespread workforce. If you do not have a home computer, you can access LIFELines at the Family Service Center and at most base libraries, as well as through your spouses's command. This is a great asset for the navy spouse and you should get on-line and explore as soon as you can.

Smooth Sailing

While the practical matters we have discussed in this chapter may seem a little complicated at first, you will be surprised how easy it is to deal with them when you take the first step: getting organized. A good filing system can solve almost any problem.

And fortunately, the second step is equally simple: ask for help. If you don't understand some aspect of the medical, dental, legal, financial, or other issues that pop up in your navy life, just call the ombudsman, NFSC, or NLSO. You will find many friendly people who will help you solve your problem and keep you sailing smoothly along.

4
Stormy Weather

The winds and waves are always on the side of the ablest navigators.
The Decline and Fall of the Roman Empire
Edward Gibbon

Don't give up the ship.

James Lawrence, Captain in *Chesapeake*

Any navy spouse faces occasional storms ashore, just as our sailors will face harsh weather at sea. The key to overcoming the inevitable difficulties engendered by separation and the stresses of military life is actually quite simple: know where to turn for help.

All of the military services, and especially the navy, invest a great deal of time and money into creating a viable support structure for spouses. There is a wide variety of agencies, service centers, ombudsmen, chaplain centers, and support groups that can provide vital and timely support during periods of separation and stress. Some are formally linked to the navy itself, some to the individual command within the navy, and some are more informal in nature. While they serve the navy spouses who turn to them in varying ways, all share a common goal of providing quality support in a timely and friendly fashion—and they generally succeed admirably.

Ombudsmen

The key to the entire navy spouse support system is the individual command ombudsmen. These trained and willing volunteers are there to answer your questions and provide information that can lead to a solution to your problems. Ombudsmen are usually experienced spouses of one of the active-duty members of the command to which your spouse is attached, and they are personally selected by the CO after a formal interview process. They also go through a detailed training program provided by the navy, which consists of a series of lectures set up by the NFSC.

Ombudsmen are official representatives of navy families, and they play a critical role in establishing effective communications between the families and the command. They also ensure that information on the command's schedule and activities is provided to the families, and they provide informal counsel and advice on the day-to-day needs of the spouses in the command. They can direct you to specialists for help in matters ranging from minor inconveniences to major problems.

When your spouse reports to a new command, you should automatically be provided with the ombudsman's name and telephone number. If for some reason you are not, your spouse can obtain the name and number from the command master chief or the administrative office. Once you learn the ombudsman's name and number, give him or her a call and introduce yourself. Make sure you are included in the command's telephone tree and that the ombudsman knows the names and ages of your children, your current address, and home and work numbers in case of emergencies involving the command.

Ombudsmen are knowledgeable about navy matters, particularly those pertaining to your spouse's command. They are sincere and attentive listeners and are trained to treat your discussions with total confidentiality. They participate in regional meetings with other command ombudsmen to share ideas and resources, and they are particularly expert in the many services offered at the NFSC.

Another important service the command ombudsman provides is the maintenance of a locating file (sometimes called a recall bill) on all the families. Whenever you move, change telephone numbers, or travel out of town for more than a week, you should make sure the ombudsman knows how to contact you. This will allow the ombudsman to keep you fully informed of schedule changes, upcoming events, or any emergencies. The recall bill information, as well as anything discussed with the ombudsman, is always held in complete confidence.

A final thought: when dealing with ombudsmen, remember that they are unpaid volunteers available to offer advice and support. They are not equipped, trained, or tasked to solve your problems themselves—but they can direct you to the right people.

Navy Family Service Centers

After your command ombudsman, the most important resource for any navy spouse is the Navy Family Service Center. Located in all major fleet centers, these professionally staffed and funded activities offer an enormous range of services and support mechanisms for navy spouses. An initial stop at the local NFSC is *mandatory* after moving to a new area.

The basic mission of the Family Service Centers is to provide counseling and general support for active duty sailors and their family members. There are fifty-five of these wonderful centers worldwide, and they range from multiple centers in the larger fleet concentration areas such as San Diego (three) and Norfolk–Virginia Beach (seven) to smaller remote centers in far-flung sites like Manama, Bahrain, and Keflavík, Iceland. A chart with their current locations is provided at the end of this section.

The NFSCs support the fleet through four essential services: Operational Support, Mobility Support, Counseling and Advocacy, and Management and Technology. The NFSCs also send representatives to homeward bound fleet ships, squadrons, and submarines. Presentations on "Return and Reunion" issues that might arise when your spouse comes home from a long deployment run the gamut from "how to buy a used car" to "reestablishing intimacy" to "handling the new baby."

The following are a few examples of the important services NFSCs provide:

- Referral and information about every aspect of a local area, from maps to lists of restaurants to key telephone numbers.

- Seminars and information on financial education. The NFSC offers programs to help individual service members, spouses, or families develop a budget, organize their financial lives, and develop basic money management skills.

- Parent education programs. These will give navy spouses up-to-date information on every aspect of child development and nurturing, including nutrition, child health, building self-esteem in your child, budgeting for children, disciplining the child, and communication between parent and children.

- Counseling services, which are at the heart of the NFSC programs. They provide individual client attention and match needs to resources for short-term one-on-one counseling, group sessions, and further referrals.

- The means to involve yourself in volunteer work. Participating in volunteer programs can make a navy spouse feel far more worthwhile and connected to the community. The NFSC provides ways to be involved in volunteer work at appropriate levels for each spouse—and this means ways to improve job skills, meet others in the community, and make new friends.

- The Spouse Employment Assistance Program (SEAP). This unique and exceptional program provides assistance to spouses looking for work. Services generally include job search workshops, a list of local job openings, a library of employment reference books and magazines, and one-on-one employment counseling.

- Relocation assistance—a key resource for navy spouses. Some of the benefits include hospitality kits (e.g., cooking and eating utensils, roll-away beds, irons, high chairs, and cribs), enrollment in Navy Information School or classes for those new to the area, a library of welcome-aboard packages from bases all over the country, and workshops to prepare you for overseas transfer.

• Stress management seminars. Managing stress is vital for navy spouses who move frequently and face many unique challenges. The NFSC seminars help you cope with these stresses. A related program is called Building Effective Anger Management Skills (BEAM), which is a six-week skill-building program for active-duty military members that helps participants develop coping strategies for stress and anger.

• The Family Advocacy Program (FAP). It offers training in how to deal with and protect yourself from family violence, including legal issues, community responses, and the navy's role in preventing and handling domestic violence.

The best stop a new navy spouse can make in his or her new community is at the NFSC. You will find friendly, motivated workers whose first question will be, "How can we help you?"

American Red Cross

One of the oldest and best structured of all international aid organizations, the American Red Cross can be a source of great help to navy spouses. This organization works closely with all of the armed services to help with everything from notifying your navy spouse of an emergency while he or she is under way to providing recreation and information programs covering general health issues.

American Red Cross services are provided by both paid and volunteer staff members, and they are available twenty-four hours a day to help in an emergency. Some of their many services include the following:

• Emergency communications to your spouse's command when illness, death, or any family emergency strikes. A message can be dispatched from any Red Cross service center and, with verification from a physician, can set in motion the wheels of an emergency leave procedure that will bring your spouse home in times of true crisis.

• Sending messages, when you have not heard from your spouse and are worried, merely to inquire about his or her general health and welfare.

• Providing emergency funds. The Red Cross can help in this area, along with the NMCRS, especially when natural disaster strikes.

Table 4.1. Navy Family Service Centers

Classification	Locations	
Regional[a]		
Jacksonville	Jacksonville, Fla. Kings Bay, Fla.	Mayport, Fla.
Hampton Roads	Little Creek, Va. Norfolk, Va. Northwest, Va.	Oceana and Dam Neck, Va. Yorktown and Newport News, Va.
Northeast	New London, Conn.	Newport, R.I.
Northwest		
East Sound	Everett, Wash.	
North Sound	Whidbey Island, Wash.	
West Sound	Bangor, Wash.	Bremerton, Wash.
Pearl Harbor	Pearl Harbor, Hawaii	Wahiawa, Hawaii
Pensacola	Pensacola, Fla.	Whiting Field, Fla.
San Diego	North Island, Calif. Point Loma, Calif.	San Diego, Calif.
South Texas	Corpus Christi, Tex. Ingleside, Tex.	Kingsville, Tex.
Heartland[b]	Annapolis, Md. Atlanta, Ga. Brunswick, Me. Charleston, S.C. Dahlgren, Va. Earle, Ark. Fort Meade, Md. Fort Worth, Tx. Great Lakes, Ill. Gulfport, Miss. Lemoore, Calif. Memphis, Tenn.	Meridian, Miss. Monterey, Calif. New Orleans, La. Pascagoula, Miss. Patuxent River, Md. Point Mugu, Calif. Port Hueneme, Calif. Saratoga Springs, N.Y. Ventura County, Calif. Washington, D.C. Willow Grove, Pa.
OCONUS and Remote[c]	Atsugi, Japan Bahrain China Lake, Ariz. Fallon, Nev. Gaeta, Italy Guam Guantánamo Bay, Cuba Keflavík, Iceland Key West, Fla.	La Maddalena, Italy London, U.K. Naples, Italy Roosevelt Roads, P.R. Rota, Spain Sasebo, Japan Sigonella, Italy Yokosuka, Japan
Satellite[d]	Lakehurst, N.J.	St. Mawgan, U.K.

Source: U.S. Navy

[a] Multiple centers in the larger fleet concentration areas

[b] Full-service centers located within U.S. borders

[c] Full-service centers in remote locations or located beyond U.S. borders

[d] Kiosk-like services

- Providing other emergency needs. In the event of a natural disaster while your spouse is under way, the Red Cross can provide services ranging from shelter to hot meals. They can also set up a location for families to meet, or to provide medical and even child care.

- Health and safety courses, health information, and referral and patient advocacy, as well as volunteer opportunities and even employment.

Contacting the Red Cross is easy. They usually have a local office at all major navy bases, often with twenty-four-hour service at large bases. Your command ombudsman will certainly have the numbers, as will the CO and XO spouses. The numbers are also listed in the local telephone directory, and an 800 number can be obtained from national directory assistance at 1-800-555-1212.

When you call the Red Cross, make sure that you have the full name of your spouse or the service member concerned, as well as his or her rate/rank, social security number, and full name and address of the command. Have your spouse write this information down and include it in your "emergency file" before he or she sails. If medical issues are involved, the Red Cross will want the name and telephone number of the attending physician to verify the information. The physician's written verification of any medical condition, which will be sent by the Red Cross to the command at no cost to you, will enable your spouse's CO to initiate emergency leave if the situation warrants and the operational schedule permits.

Navy–Marine Corps Relief Society

A private, nonprofit organization, the Navy–Marine Corps Relief Society is the ultimate "safety net" for navy spouses. It collects donations from every sailor and marine annually to establish a fund to "take care of our own." Volunteers staff the offices of the NMCRS, and they can help with a variety of needs, from a short-term loan to disaster relief. They can provide a combination of conventional loans, grants, or interest-free loans to help "tide over" spouses having a hard time. Please note that they work to ensure that individuals receiving loans are responsible and that the loan funds are used for essential purchases such as food, shelter, clothes, and so forth. Some authorized reasons for loans might include

> emergency transportation
> food, rent, and utilities
> disaster relief
> personal needs when paychecks are delayed
> emergency repairs of automobiles

The NMCRS also provides education loans for dependent children, spouses, and fleet inputs to commissioning programs; visiting nurses for housebound retirees, widows and widowers, and mothers with newborns; and layettes for expectant mothers. And it operates nonprofit thrift shops on many bases, with proceeds going toward the NMCRS fund.

Getting in touch with the NMCRS is simple. As with the Red Cross, your command ombudsman and the spouses of the CO and XO will have the number. You should also find it in the base telephone directory.

Chaplains

A special resource in times of emergency are the superb navy chaplains. All of them are fully qualified ministers, and many are experienced counselors with thousands of hours of practical experience dealing with navy problems and the emergencies of life. No matter what their denomination, they are always available to the navy spouse for religious or spiritual guidance, counseling, and practical assistance.

Your command ombudsman can put you in touch with a navy chaplain, and most bases have a chaplain's center—normally located with the base chapel—with offices and counseling times available. Chaplains work closely with the NFSC, the NMCRS, the American Red Cross, and other community programs. They can make referrals for health, financial, professional, or emergency leave problems. They are often willing to make visits to the home and even the workplace—truly a wonderful group of people who are a reliable resource for navy spouses.

Commanding Officer and Executive Officer Spouses

After your command ombudsman, the best source of valid information will be the spouses of the CO and XO. Generally, they will have been with the navy for a long time, and are of course in touch with the top two decision makers in the command on a regular basis. They will have seen a wide variety of emergencies during their spouses' careers, and thus have a wealth of experience to share. These spouses are also able to communicate with shore-based decision makers who can help resolve problems and provide information.

Bear in mind, however, that the CO and XO spouses *may not* have a great deal of navy experience if they are relatively new to the marriage themselves. Likewise, they may not live in the same geographic area of the command or simply may not be particularly involved in navy issues because of their busy careers or concerns. Each command is different in this regard, and your ombudsman can give you a sense of CO and XO spouse involvement at your sailor's command. As a rule, you should *always* attempt to contact the command ombudsman *before* getting in touch with either the CO's or XO's spouse.

In general, however, most CO/XO spouses are involved and helpful people with a great deal of experience. They can be a valuable resource in times of emergency if you cannot contact the ombudsman for some reason.

Emergency Leave

When things *really* go wrong on the home front, it may be time to find out whether or not your spouse can obtain emergency leave from the command. The navy has set guidelines for granting emergency leave, and it is often difficult to arrange. Bear in mind that the system will make every fair effort to get your spouse home if the emergency warrants, but occasionally operations and distance may make it impossible. The CO, who must make the often-difficult decision as to whether your spouse is permitted to go on emergency leave, is authorized to do so by the navy under the following conditions. (Keep in mind that emergency leave usually is granted—provided the military situation permits—when the existence of an emergency has been determined by letter, telegram, or telephone call from the family member, minister, or attending physician as verified by the Red Cross.)

- when the service member's return will contribute to the welfare of a dying immediate family member (the service member's or spouse's father, mother, person standing in loco parentis [someone who raised the individual], spouse, children, brother, sister, or only living relative)

- upon the death of an immediate family member (service member's or spouse's)

- when an accident to or serious illness of an immediate family member (service member's or spouse's) results in a significant family problem and imposes important responsibilities on the service member that must be met immediately and that cannot be accomplished from the member's duty station or by any other individual or means

- when failure of the service member to return home would create a severe and unusual hardship on either the member or his or her family.

In general, if your spouse is deployed overseas, the navy will fund travel back to the continental United States. If you live overseas, funding is likewise available for your spouse to return to the United States for emergencies. Families often can obtain space-available transportation on military flights to accompany the service member. Inquire at the air transportation terminal of your closest military base.

Emergency Communications

In an emergency, the first thought of any navy spouse is, "How do I get in touch with my sailor?" Fortunately, the navy provides several means to do just that, and, depending on the nature of the emergency, the communications can be virtually instantaneous.

Ombudsmen

The first stop, as always, is the command ombudsman. If for some reason you are unable to get in touch with the ombudsman and it is a true emergency, call the CO's or XO's spouse. Both will have the ship's International Maritime Satellite (Inmarsat) telephone numbers, which provide a means to pick up a telephone and call the ship anywhere, anytime. This option can be used only in the case of a true emergency, such as a death in the family, a life-threatening illness, a major accident leading to hospitalization, a natural disaster, and so forth. The ombudsman, who deals with many problems, will be able to evaluate your situation and decide whether an Inmarsat call is necessary. (The CO and XO spouses can also evaluate the necessity of this type of call in the ombudsman's absence.)

Red Cross

In certain circumstances, the Red Cross will be willing to send an emergency message. Again, this option is reserved for serious emergencies similar to those requiring Inmarsat telephone calls. The Red Cross office in your area will determine whether your emergency qualifies, and your ombudsman can offer advice on this option. Before you call the Red Cross, be sure to have your spouse's full name, social security number, division, and ship. There is no charge for this service.

Electronic Mail

The best and quickest method to maintain day-to-day communication with your sailor is generally by e-mail. If you have not entered the electronic age and your spouse will be going to sea on a regular basis, then now is the time to learn! The good news is that the navy will help you get on-line and maintain electronic communication with your sailor even if you don't have a home computer. You should, however, save for a personal computer and get on-line from your home as soon as you can.

E-mail connectivity is generally available for sailors, depending on operational constraints and security issues. On most of the ships in the

Deployments in the Electronic Age
By Laurie Capen

If you've been associated with the Navy long, then you know the painful feelings when your sailor goes to sea. Whether it is for six weeks or six months, it can be difficult to know how to handle communications with your sailor, especially in this information age.

There was a time somewhere between the age of dinosaurs and the a vent of Microsoft when communications during deployment went something like this: The ship left and you began writing daily. You ran to the mailbox every day checking for mail and felt a little embarrassed since you knew you would see nothing for at least the first month. You numbered every letter since they inevitably arrived at the ship in random order. Your sailor would find out Fluffy was now going to be fine in letter number ten only to receive letter number two several weeks later describing Fluffy's encounter with the neighborhood dog. Phone calls were very infrequent and either your phone bill rivaled your rent payment, or you ended every side of the conversation with the word "Over," as a third party was monitoring the call. There was no way to consult your sailor about most decisions so after reunion came the sometimes awkward task of trying to explain everything that had occurred since your sailor left, especially your out of control phone bill.

Happily, communications during deployment have improved dramatically. The advent of e-mail has revolutionized these communications and is a huge boost to morale. Return and reunion is a much smoother transition for families as the sense of "disconnectedness" is reduced from the increased communication during deployment. However, there are some pitfalls families should be aware of.

Responses to e-mail are usually less than 24 hours and now the preferred means of communicating while the ship is away. It offers the opportunity to include the deployed sailor in almost all decisions. This can be very comforting and alleviate the sense of loneliness to know you can get input on almost any subject.

Children can be included in e-mail as well with the youngest dictating to the parent what they wish to express. My husband was able to send occasional photographs on the e-mail and would occasionally e-mail each of the children separately, contributing greatly to their feeling connected to their Dad.

On the flip side, there are some pitfalls to be avoided. The spouse left behind needs to be aware that the sailor still feels helpless to change problems. As a result, constant negativity should be avoided. It may be better to share Fluffy's mishap after you've been to the vet and have a solution.

Make sure to share the positives going on as well as the problems. No matter how bad it seems, there is always something positive to share. Sharing just the negative can contribute to feelings of guilt and helplessness. Sharing only the positive, however, can make the sailor feel as if he or she is not needed. Balance and good judgment are key. One time while my sailor was at sea, my son's doctor wanted to perform surgery on his eye for a slight deformity. The situation was not life threatening, so I told the doctor I would wait until I could communicate with my husband.

A word of caution is necessary here about family tragedies. Never, ever inform your sailor about a death in the family by using e-mail. You must use the Red Cross message system. Although slower and more difficult to use, it ensures that your sailor is informed by someone trained to handle grief situations, such as the chaplain. It is also the only way to have your sailor sent home if the situation warrants it. Even if you think it is a distant relative, please call the ombudsman and Red Cross. I would even reserve the death of a pet to a phone call in a port versus e-mail. I would not want my husband going to stand watch or perform any other duty requiring his full concentration after reading a disturbing e-mail.

Privacy is always a scarce commodity on the ship, and it should not be assumed that e-mail is private. There is generally a line waiting to use the computers with e-mail, and there may be people looking over the sailor's shoulder. There are some communications that are still better left to good old-fashioned "snail mail."

For security or operational reasons, there are times when the e-mail needs to be shut down on the ship. This can cause unnecessary panic among families. We can get spoiled very quickly by the ability to communicate so rapidly. This is nothing to be concerned about and it is done for our sailor's protection. Go back to writing the old-fashioned letters and the e-mail will be back up in no time. Also, sometimes operations get too intense and maybe the sailor cannot get to the computer for a couple days. Don't read anything into this other than your sailor is very busy.

Phone calls, although still infrequent in the information age, are not as rushed and stressful as there is regular communication via e-mail. I remember during early deployments keeping a notepad by my bed so when the 3:00 A.M. call would come, I could quickly recite all the information I needed to pass on and maybe have two minutes for personal conversation after all the family business was taken care of. With e-mail, phone calls could focus more on the relationship and were much more relaxed (and cheaper as we did not have to waste time on business things).

I have to make a small confession. As much as I love the ability to communicate so freely with my husband during deployment, a little romance is lost in e-mail. I have bundles of letters tied together from our "dinosaur deployments" that record our every handwritten thought and feeling. These are among my most treasured possessions. I have no such record from our "electronic deployment." Although I did send some handwritten letters during this last deployment, they lack the same sense of urgency and heart-felt communication from earlier deployments. I would encourage those left behind to still get the stationery out and send the handwritten letter as if it was the only communication you would ever have. Your marriage will be better for it.

fleet, you will exchange e-mail with your sailor about 75 percent of the time. You usually can expect to send an email and receive a response within twenty-four hours, unless there are specific operational reasons to close down the electronic mail. This would include potential contingency operations such as an upcoming Tomahawk launch or the evacuation of civilians from an embassy, for example.

In addition to differences in operational schedules, you need to understand that ships in the fleet will differ in terms of e-mail capabilities. Larger ships, such as aircraft carriers and large-deck amphibious ships, have the means to provide e-mail services on a faster basis with less downtime. Today, all but the smallest ships possess at least the basic resources to process e-mails in a batch method (USOGrams) to keep you connected with your sailor.

On the homefront, there are specific navy base locations for e-mail computer banks, and this will be thoroughly explained at predeployment briefings. If you are newly arrived at a command, the ombudsman will be able to explain to you on a one-on-one basis how you can get on-line with your sailor. This information is also available in base newspapers, on command web sites, including the naval station where your sailor's ship is based, and at Family Service Centers, where you may have the ability to contact your sailor twenty-four hours a day, seven days a week.

A personal computer will be less than $1,000, and you can receive assistance from the Family Service Center in activating a free e-mail account. Today there are also options to purchase relatively inexpensive home terminals that are not really computers, but rather, e-mail and Internet-connection devices priced at $300 or less. Admittedly, these are all significant investments but buying one is a good idea for the navy family that wants to stay connected with their loved one.

When sending e-mail, all of the normal suggestions for communication with your deployed spouse apply: Be supportive, do not spread rumors, stay upbeat, don't make troubles seem larger than they are, and please don't come across feeling sorry for yourself. On the other hand, you should not hide difficulties and challenges—especially if you need help to solve them. Many of the problems we faced with deployed sailors in the 1970s and 1980s—such as pay accounts, allotments, and other financial issues—can be quickly resolved because of the connectivity of e-mail.

One issue that you should recognize is that electronic mail is not a private communication in the way a letter is. Generally speaking, e-mail *is* quite private, but be aware that some ships pass e-mail through a processing center. Be cautious in the personal detail, the discussion of personal affection, and keep your prose appropriate to the situation. Save those really passionate thoughts for the total privacy of a letter!

Western Union

If you have an emergency that is not disastrous but still worthy of quick communication, your next best choice is a Western Union telegram. You can outline the problem in a few words and tell your sailor to call, and this message can be delivered overnight in most cases. You can send these quite inexpensively (generally less than twenty dollars), and they will reach your sailor quickly. This type of communication would be appropriate when you are having financial problems, when it has been some time since you have heard from your spouse and you are consequently worried, or if you have an urgent need to communicate your travel plans or location. You can find Western Union in the telephone book, or you can call them at 1-800-325-6000. Do remember that many people will see your telegram, including the CO and XO, so always maintain a reasonable and professional tone. An e-mail may be just as swift, but this is an option if e-mail is down.

USOGram

Another means of emergency communication that is rapid and is popular with those who do not have e-mail is the USOGram. Most large navy bases have a USOGram center where you can very inexpensively (two to three dollars) send about 150–300 words to your spouse while he or she is out at sea. These are generally delivered within two or three days in a telegram-like format and are quite reliable. This would be a good method of communication for special days like anniversaries, birthdays, and celebrations, when you want something faster than a letter but less expensive than a telegram. You can find the location of the USOGram office through your command ombudsman, although for the most part these are being phased out and replaced by e-mail.

Letters

The most inexpensive and generally reliable method, of course, is a good old-fashioned letter. These are delivered to your sailor anywhere from five to twenty days after you drop it at the post office, depending on the ship's schedule and location. It costs only the going rate for delivery in the United States despite the fact that your letter is often sent by the navy over many thousands of miles. Some of your letters will travel ten thousand miles on their way to a sailor in the Persian Gulf, for example. And sailors love nothing more than mail. The drawback from an emergency standpoint, obviously, is the time lag. Remember that any special mail service such as special delivery, overnight mail, or two-day air mail

USOGRAM - USOGRAM - USOGRAM - USOGRAM
USS Arleigh Burke (DDG-51)

20 May 2001

From: SK2 Samantha Smith, S-3 Division

To: Mr. William Watkins
        1014 San Pedro Drive
        Alexandria, VA 22301

Dear Billy,

I'm so happy to have these USOGRAMs, so we can keep in touch during this deployment. I hated to leave you and the kids yesterday on the pier, but I'm really proud to be deploying on a great ship like Arleigh Burke. I'll send you a USOGRAM at least once a week.

The captain got on the 1MC this morning and told us what the schedule in the Mediterranean looks like. Everyone is really psyched up! We'll be going to Rota, Spain, first, just to top off with some supplies. Then on to the coast of Spain to do some exercises with some NATO navies. Our first liberty port should be Toulon, France. Then we'll be going to Italy. I've heard Naples is OK, although the XO says it will probably be a working port since we'll be in for almost ten days. I can't give you the exact dates yet because of security, but I'll call from each port when we pull in.

I checked with the Disbursing guys, and they said the split allotment will work fine from my pay. I should have plenty of money for liberty. I'm going to try and buy some dolls for the girls in France, and maybe pick up a nice leather wallet for you in Italy.

Please give my Mom and Dad a call, and let them know you've heard from me already. I know they'll want to hear how you and the kids are doing without me.

You know how much I love you. . . . I'll try to send separate USOGRAMS to Kelli and Kathi tomorrow. Lots of love and kisses, and I can't wait to see you again at Thanksgiving. Only 178 days and a wake up!

I love you. Always, Sam

USOGrams are a good way to keep in touch during deployments if e-mail is not available.

is not recognized by the fleet post office. Paying extra will not speed up your mail service, unfortunately.

A good approach to dealing with an emergency is to use a combination of methods, perhaps sending an e-mail, USOGram, or even a telegram and then following it up with a long letter and more documentation as appropriate via mail. Again, your command ombudsman can best advise you as to which combination to use and which will meet your needs.

Other Methods of Communication

A specialized method of communication, which must be initiated from the ship, is a military affiliated radio system, or MARS, call. This is the use of high-frequency radio waves to connect to a shore station in the continental United States. The stateside operator, normally a ham radio volunteer, will then place a collect call to your home. This call may come from anywhere; for example, your spouse may be randomly connected with a radio operator in Idaho, thus the collect call to your home in Florida then would be fairly expensive. It is still a good deal, however, because you can talk to your spouse from far away and while the command is under way—something that is normally impossible. Remember that the call is monitored by the ham radio operator and therefore is not very private. You must say "over" when you want your spouse to answer, and you cannot reveal the ship's name, talk about specific port visits, or discuss the ship's mission. It is a polite practice to thank the MARS operator (who is a volunteer) for his or her help in setting up the call. If you send a telegram asking your spouse to contact you, a MARS call may be the quickest way for him or her to do so.

A fairly new means of communicating with your sailor is the cellular telephone. It can be very handy, especially when the ship is operating near the coast. Unfortunately, cellular telephones don't reach beyond thirty to fifty miles from land—but navy ships are often within that range. Your sailor will need to purchase the cellular telephone, although some ships are buying several of them and making them available to crew members for use with calling cards. Have your sailor check with his or her command about the policy and availability of cellular telephone communication.

The world of telecommunications is constantly evolving these days. I would guess that within five years there will be inexpensive, reliable, commercial telephone contact with every ship in the fleet. This will go a long way toward improving quality of life in the fleet, and will also help defuse many emergencies quickly. Watch for improvements in this

It is always possible that your spouse could end up in a combat situation. Pacific Test Center.

area over the next few years, and in the meantime, use all of the different means of communications to "stay in touch" with your sailor.

Combat Operations, Accidents, and Media Relations

A unique challenge faced by navy spouses is the very real possibility that their husbands or wives may find themselves in a combat situation. This is understandably a frightening experience for spouses back home, and the best way to react is to gather as much information as possible and stay calm.

As always, the command ombudsman will receive regular updates, operations permitting, from the CO. These will be passed along to the families through the ombudsman "Careline," a recorded message that can usually be accessed by dialing the ombudsman's line. Additionally, most commands will try to arrange briefings for the spouses at home, normally conducted by the local public affairs officers. These briefings will be publicized through the ombudsman.

Remember, if your spouse is involved in combat operations, the U.S. Navy is *by far* the best equipped, trained, and motivated fighting force at sea in the world—this is not bragging; it is simply fact. Your spouse will be very safe, and the CO and chain of command will do everything possible to ensure that the unit—be it a ship, submarine, aircraft squadron, or SEAL team—is used in a safe, intelligent manner in combat.

Sometimes operations at sea have dangers other than combat. Very rarely, ships collide with each other or run aground. While distressing to all involved, these incidents almost never lead to a loss of life or danger to your sailor. If something like this involves your spouse's ship, the families will be contacted and briefed on the situation by the ombudsman.

Unfortunately, sometimes such incidents—whether combat or bad accidents—lead to encounters with the media. You may find yourself asked to comment on "how you feel" about your spouse's involvement in such a situation. If you are contacted by the media, the best course of action is simple: decline to talk to them. Remember, you are *never* under any obligation to talk to the media. If they persist, refer them to the navy office of public affairs, a corps of professional public relations officers. Their number is available from your command ombudsman.

If for some reason you become involved in a discussion with media people, remember at a minimum *never* to discuss your spouse's operations, schedule, or mission. Such things are probably classified, and revealing them in an open press may actually endanger your and others' loved ones as they fulfill their important missions.

Hurricanes and Other Natural Disasters

One of the best things about being a navy spouse is that you often will live within a few miles of the ocean, with all the recreation and natural beauty of coastal living at your disposal. On the other hand, being close to the shoreline in a navy port can put you directly in the path of one of nature's most erratic and dangerous weather phenomena, the hurricane.

The good news is that with today's forecasting techniques and mass media reporting, you probably will have at least several days' notice before a hurricane bears down on your town. The bad news is that your sailor may be at sea, conducting what the navy calls "hurricane evasion."

When a hurricane approaches a navy port, the chain of command watches it very closely, and about forty-eight hours before a predicted land strike in the vicinity of the base, they generally will order a sortie either out to sea (for ships and submarines) or to an inland location (for the aircraft). Ships and submarines are designed to ride out storms comfortably at sea, whereas they are at high risk when tied up in port during a truly strong hurricane. The one-hundred-plus mile-per-hour winds that come with the biggest hurricanes can snap the lines that tie ships and submarines to the piers, destroy the piers themselves, and cause billions of dollars in damage to expensive ships. Aircraft likewise can be swept up and destroyed.

With your sailor out evading the hurricane, you would be placed in the uncomfortable position of having to deal with the approaching storm without his or her support. Fortunately, most bases will have help and advice readily available to you. A few points to bear in mind during hurricane season (roughly June through November):

- Listen to the media for warnings. On television, CNN and the Weather Channel are good sources. The newspapers generally will run a tracking map that can help sort out the path of the storm, and they will provide a prehurricane checklist for homeowners and apartment dwellers alike.

- Always evade and never attempt to ride out a coming storm. The best plan is to board up windows, stow outside gear inside the garage or house, and drive to a friend's house or a motel well outside of the predicted storm path. (But be sure to check in with the ombudsman before leaving. He or she can usually give advice on how to prepare.) Store water in the house before you leave—if you can return and the water if still cut off, you will need this.

- Before you return to the house, make sure you have plenty of bottled drinking water, flashlights, a portable radio, batteries, and canned goods. A heating source (canned heat or a camping stove) is also a good idea. And be prepared to "camp out" in your own house for the days before electricity and water are restored.

- Most ships, if required to hurricane sortie, will leave a detachment of male sailors in port to help out spouses. The navy base also will have help available.

One key piece of advice for the navy spouse facing a hurricane: don't worry about your sailor. The navy tracks the storms very carefully, and the ships, submarines, and aircraft are well designed to operate in the worst of seas very safely. The units also receiving constant updates on the storm and recommended courses to take them to safety. Your job is to concentrate on the home front and make sure that you, your family, and other navy spouses remaining ashore are well protected and out of danger.

Rumors

Particularly during emergency situations, rumors can be one of the worst things to happen to navy spouses. Whenever there is no valid, officially provided information, rumors can run rampant. When you hear something from *anyone* other than the command ombudsman or the CO and XO spouses, you should consider it a rumor and refuse to repeat it. Some examples of rumors that can escalate to pseudo-emergencies:

"I heard the ship is going to the Persian Gulf and might have to extend on cruise."

"They say there is a big drug ring on the ship, and lots of people are getting busted [punished] at captain's mast" [disciplinary hearing for minor infractions].

"I understand that lots of the guys are running around on their wives in Naples."

Two suggestions for stopping rumors in their tracks: first, always ask others what their source is for a statement if it sounds like a rumor. If they have not heard it from the ombudsman or the CO and XO spouses, it is a rumor and is probably inaccurate or untrue. Tell them that. Second, if someone else persists in spreading stories and rumors, ask if you can quote him or her and verify it with the command ombudsman.

Rumors can hurt people and are especially dangerous in times of emergency, combat operations, or when accidents occur at sea. Don't put up with rumors.

Emergency File

When your sailor is assigned to sea duty, you should always maintain an emergency file in your desk. It does not need to be large or bulky, but it should contain the following:

- your sailor's full name, social security number, date of birth, and exact assignment within the command

- your sailor's will and a power of attorney if one has been executed (see chapter 3 for details on these topics)

- the command's mailing address and telephone numbers while in port (which may change frequently due to movements to different piers), and the ombudsman's telephone number and address

- telephone numbers for the local American Red Cross, the NMCRS, the NFSC, and Western Union; many NFSCs have handy wallet-sized cards with these and dozens of other valuable local telephone numbers

- other key telephone numbers for your command as available, such as the CO/XO/command master chief spouses and the family support group chairperson

- any emergency pamphlets or information from the NFSC, such as literature on hurricanes and coping with stress, and emergency babysitting services

You should go over this information about once a month and make sure it is updated. If you are unable find something, call the ombudsman and ask for help. You and your sailor should review this file in detail before any extended operations (more than thirty days away from home).

Personal Security

To weather successfully the storms that come along in navy life, you must have a clear understanding of personal security. In addition to the items discussed here, your NFSC will have other literature and classes available to help ensure that you are safe while your sailor is at sea.

Around the house, make sure the locks are secure and that no previous dweller still has access. If you are renting, discuss this issue with your landlord. Make sure the exterior of your home is well lit and that shrubbery is trimmed back. Your home should be burglar-proofed through a variety of means, including strong locks with dead bolts, wooden dowels at the base of sliding glass doors and above windows, and an inspection by the local police department. (Most have home security programs that will provide an officer to do a security check on your house —take advantage of it, especially if your spouse will be out at sea a great deal.) For deployments, you may also want to consider an alarm system, which can be purchased and installed by your sailor or procured through a commercial service. While expensive, they can provide significant peace of mind, especially if you live in an area with a high crime rate.

When you have people come to the house for deliveries or repairs, be sure to check their identification before opening the door. Install and use a peephole for this purpose. Never open the door to a stranger who is soliciting, and if someone requests use of your telephone, direct them to a public telephone or offer to call, but never open the door. List only initials on mailboxes at apartment houses, and consider owning a dog— even small ones offer good protection if they bark at strangers. Never let strangers know your spouse's schedule. Be cautious.

If you are going to take a trip while your spouse is out at sea, consider leaving a house key with a trusted neighbor who can watch the house. Be sure to stop delivery of the newspaper and mail, and set a timer on an inside light so it will appear someone is home. Another option is to ask your neighbor to come in each evening, check overall security, and turn on a light. Never simply leave an outside light burning all day and night—you may as well hang a "Welcome Aboard" sign for any burglars. You also should make arrangements for someone to mow your lawn, and if you alert the police to your absence, they will periodically check the house.

There are additional personal safety precautions you should take whenever you are away from home. When going from your car to the house and back, always carry your keys in your hand, ready to use. Always look in your car before entering it. Walk purposefully from place to place, and avoid dark areas and paths with heavy shrubbery. Always be alert to your surroundings and maintain situational awareness. Keep doors locked and windows up while driving, especially through urban areas with stoplights. Park near entrances to stores, and if it is late, ask at the store if a security guard is available to walk you to your car, or leave with a group of other shoppers. Avoid strange neighborhoods when driving at night, and let someone know when you are out of the house in the evening if you are alone at home. If you are being followed, don't go home—drive instead to a police or fire station. Finally, remember that the things you learned in kindergarten still apply today: don't talk to strangers and never accept a ride from someone whom you don't know well.

If, despite your precautions, you are confronted, try to stay calm. You can talk your way out of many bad situations. Don't be afraid to make a scene, call for help, blow a whistle, or otherwise let people in the vicinity know you are in danger. If you are physically or sexually assaulted, remember that your first priority is to escape with the least amount of psychological and physical injury. Following an assault, go to a safe place and call the police emergency number and report the attack. Don't do anything that will change the crime scene, and don't initiate any personal hygienic procedures—you will destroy physical evidence. The police will handle your case and provide assistance. Many cities have sexual assault hot lines to put you in touch with helpful resources. Your command ombudsman can also provide help.

Car Problems

Perhaps the most common and irritating problem navy spouses face while their sailors are at sea is car trouble. It is uncanny how cars seem to "know" when your sailor is under way and choose that moment to break down, generally at the most inconvenient times.

To avoid this problem, first make sure is that your cars have up-to-date base stickers. These can be obtained at the base pass and ID office and are provided free of charge. They will identify your vehicle and permit unrestricted access to any naval facility. To obtain a sticker, you will need a valid military ID card, the vehicle's registration, a valid driver's license, a current state inspection sticker, and proof of insurance. When your sailor is deploying, double-check to make sure the sticker is valid throughout the cruise. Also make sure you have all of the appropriate documentation in one place, along with an extra car key.

Next, you should become familiar with the basics of your cars. Make sure you understand what type of gasoline is used, how often the oil and filter should be changed and when it was last done (generally every three to five thousand miles), when lubrication should be performed (same time as the oil and filter change), the basic maintenance schedule (found in the car manual), when the battery was last changed (you need a new one approximately every three years), and condition of the tires and when they need replacement (tires must have at least one-quarter inch tread to be acceptable). If a deployment is coming up and your sailor is the one who works on the cars, have him or her write out a dated schedule of any work that should be done and where it should be performed. Try to find a good local mechanic, preferably close to home, for emergencies.

Learn to recognize early warning signs of car trouble. Drips from under the hood are something to be checked out, unless it is water condensing from the air conditioning. Anything that is oily or colored generally indicates a problem. When you buy gasoline, learn how to do a quick check under the hood: oil level, belts, battery, coolant. Have your sailor give you a lesson before cruise, or check out a simple car-care book from the library. In your car, you should carry a canvas tote bag with the following items: jumper cables, flashlight, distress flag, flares or reflectors, duct tape, can of pneumatic tire inflator, screwdriver, and pliers. You don't need to be an expert mechanic to avoid trouble on the highway.

Exceptional Family Member Program

Perhaps nothing is more frightening than a disability or problem with a child. The navy recognizes this and has created a special program to help. The Exceptional Family Member (EFM) Program provides support that continues wherever the family moves. It is a very helpful approach to families that face the many storms that come as they deal with their children's ongoing problems. The following information on the program comes from the program manager in Washington, D.C.:

• EFM program managers are located at major military medical facilities, the NFSC, and the Bureau of Naval Personnel. They will help you with the necessary forms.

• The National Information Center for Children and Youth with Disabilities (at 1-800-695-0285) can give you lists of special education and medical services and resources for the state in which you live.

• The TRICARE or health benefits advisor at your local military medical facility can help with medical payments. The Program for the Handicapped, a TRICARE program, will pay up to $1,000 a month for therapy, equipment, and treatment of your special-needs family members.

• Your local insurance company may offer a TRICARE supplemental policy for special-needs family members.

• Local chapters of the Easter Seal Society can refer you to early intervention programs for infants and toddlers. Some chapters also loan out special equipment for handicapped children.

• The Department of Special Education in your local school system can outline programs available for your special-needs child. In some cases there are special adult education programs available as well.

• Parents Are Vital in Education (at 1-800-572-7368) offers specialized training of military parents to help you understand special education programs.

• Department of Defense Schools (at 703-696-4386) can tell you what special education programs are offered at overseas duty stations.

• The number of the EFM program in Washington, D.C., is 1-800-527-8830.

Once enrolled in the Exceptional Family Member (EFM) program, your family will be assigned to one of six categories based upon the frequency and the duration of treatment, as well as the support that the exceptional member requires. Orders are issued using the category assignment as a guideline, although it is important to note that these categories apply to the family member and do not restrict the sea and shore duty requirements of the service member:

Category 1: Needs do not generally limit assignments
Category 2: Condition requires specific CONUS or overseas
                    locations

Category 3: Usually no assignment to overseas locations based on nonavailability of needed services

Category 4: Assignment to billets near major military or civilian medical facility

Category 5: Enables service member to homestead in a major medical area that offers both sea and shore assignments

Category 6: Temporary, condition requires a stable environment for six months to one year.

You can get more information on the EFM program from your Family Service Center. Applications are available at local branch medical clinics and at naval medical centers. The placement process takes about six weeks, and applications must be updated once every three years or whenever there is a change in condition or family status. In Hampton Roads alone, there are over three thousand navy and Marine Corps personnel taking advantage of this fine program, which helps our families through demanding challenges.

Taking Care of Yourself

As crises unfold, as they occasionally will, always remember that your most important resource is *yourself*. Every navy spouse must protect his or her own reserves of balance, judgment, and energy to respond to whatever the future holds. Watch for the following signs of "burnout":

> physical exhaustion
> irritability and a tendency to argue
> loss of accuracy in judgment
> mental "blankness"—a vague feeling of unease and depression coupled with an inability to concentrate

If you find yourself experiencing these symptoms when a crisis strikes, *take care of yourself*. Taking breaks and maintaining your personal routines (meal hours, workouts, sleep patterns) are very important. You can never take on the entire crisis by yourself—enlist help from others in the command and share such tasks as carpooling, baby-sitting, and cooking. Relaxation techniques such as listening to soothing music, meditation, breathing exercises, and working out are all valuable in helping you maintain your balance and judgment. Eat a healthy diet, with plenty of fresh fruits, vegetables, and carbohydrates (pasta, rice, breads). Try to stay away from fast food during a crisis, no matter how convenient it may be. Additionally, the command's family support group can be a great source of help and strength.

Remember, you cannot help your family or fellow navy spouses during an emergency if you are a wreck.

Summary

Emergencies will occur. And navy spouses may indeed face a few more than the average American. The good news is that the navy is standing behind you every step of the way and has a large and effective support system in place to help in times of trouble. Make use of every resource available to you. If you participate in a good support system, keep yourself up-to-speed on the command's schedule and activities, avoid people who spread rumors, and stay in touch with the ombudsman, you will be able to weather any storm that crosses your course.

A Final Note

We all know there is a certain amount of danger when one chooses a career in the navy. This was well illustrated in the October 2000 bombing of USS *Cole* by a terrorist organization in Aden, Yemen. The navy lost seventeen sailors, with thirty-nine others injured. Despite suffering terrible damage, the ship survived and has returned to service. The navy wrapped its arms around the crew and families of USS *Cole,* and the president, the secretary of defense, the chairman of the joint chiefs of staff, and the secretary of the navy spoke at the moving memorial service held in Norfolk a few days after the bombing. Secretary of the Navy Richard Danzig delivered a particularly beautiful and meaningful speech that endeavored to comfort the families of the wounded and the dead, and to the larger navy family beyond *Cole.* His words serve to remind us not only of the danger but also of the significance of a career in the navy.

America Loves Its Citizens

One of the reasons that I love America is because it loves its citizens. In other times, and on this very day in other places, people are regarded as means and not ends, as fodder, stepping-stones, dispensable assets. Because we are not like that, we grieve today. We see in the 17 people who died on October 12th 17 wonders, 17 sons and daughters. We mourn brothers and sisters, mothers, fathers, and those who will never be mothers and fathers. Seventeen unique people. We cherish them. We grieve because we could not protect them. Instead, they died protecting us.

That we live in America is, in itself, an act of grace. We came to it naturally; we were born into it. Or we were welcomed as immigrants; we were naturalized. By either route, America has been for every one of us a gift, and what a stupendous gift—a country that was built collectively but cherishes us individually; a country built of the effort of servicemen and statesmen, farmers and factory workers, those who toiled on the railroad and those who bankrolled it. Our philosophers, our politicians, our priests, all together, created something bigger than any of us; and then, they gave it to us.

Any true gift is infused with opportunity, and responsibility that arises from that opportunity. An inherent talent, a good education, money in the bank—they all cry to the recipient, What will you make of this? What will you do individually? What will we do collectively in light of how many have done so much for us?

These 17 answered that question. They didn't opt just for themselves; they didn't stay home; they didn't turn away from their country. They put themselves out there. They joined a family, the United States Navy, and the USS *Cole* (DDG-67)—a ship, the very essence of a group enterprise. And think not just of these 17. Think of the 39 who were injured, and then think of the 240 beyond them; the 240 who absorbed the shock of the explosion, who saw the death of 17, the injury of two score, but who turned to and fought on; fought together for their ship and for their shipmates.

For two days and two nights, they fought under the most extreme conditions—blood, bent and broken steel, flooding, uncertainty and danger. They saved their ship, their injured—every one of them—and each other. And then their generators failed. The waters rose, and they had to do it all over again. Waist-deep in water, manning bucket brigades by hand, they did it again. Amidst all of that, their captain said to me, "Mr. Secretary, we will save this ship. We will repair this ship. We will take this ship home and we will sail this ship again to sea."

In every gift there is a responsibility. The *Cole* has given us a gift. The 17 join more than 1.3 million service men and women who have given us their lives. Thirty-nine from the *Cole* were injured; 240 fought on. All together, they added a building block to America. Will we, as recipients of this gift, live up to them? I think we will; we're Americans.

Thank you, *Cole*.

A very beautiful tribute, and one that captures the meaning in all that the navy does.

I Attended the *Cole* Memorial

By Shannon Riggs

I didn't know any of the sailors who were lost or injured in the recent attack on the USS *Cole*. Still, I found myself grappling with whether to attend the memorial service.

My husband serves on board the USS *Dwight D. Eisenhower*. I heard on the news that the *Cole*'s injured sailors would all attend the service, as well as some of the families of those who perished.

I almost decided not to go. I didn't want to appear as if I were ogling the injured sailors and grieving families, like a rubbernecker driving past a traffic accident; I have too much respect for what these sailors and their families lost. Also, my four-year-old son, not yet in school, would have to come to the service with me. I worried that he wouldn't understand, that he might act inappropriately.

Somewhere, deeper down, I also worried that he *would* understand.

As I made my way down Hampton Boulevard toward the Navy Base, two thoughts kept crossing my mind, like the refrains of a hymn. The first was that this could have happened to my family and me. My husband had just returned from a six-month deployment. The second was that it *wasn't* me. Did I belong at this memorial service?

Still, I drove on.

When we arrived, the skies were dark gray, threatening rain. I zipped my son's bright yellow raincoat and thought the color was too bright, too cheerful. Maybe we shouldn't have come.

As we edged our way through a sea of crisp, white uniforms and somber faces, a reporter from *The New York Times* stopped me. He wanted to know if I knew any of the *Cole* sailors.

"No," I said. Then he wanted to know why I was there and why I had brought my young son with me. I looked up at my husband's ship towering over us. Just a couple of months ago, it wasn't there.

"My husband serves on board the *Eisenhower*," I said. "They just got back from deployment a couple of months ago."

But why did I feel the need to be at the ceremony, the reporter wanted to know. He merely voiced what I'd been asking myself.

"Because when my husband was out to sea, every time I baked cookies for a care package, every time I sent a love letter, what I was really saying was, 'Please, God, don't let this happen,'" I said. "And then two months ago, I stood on this pier and took part in a homecoming party. What I was really saying then was, 'Thank God this didn't happen.'" I looked at the reporter, scribbling his notes. "And now, dear God, it has happened, and I just couldn't stay home."

Then I told him what we all say. That the Navy is a big family, and we pull together in times of crisis.

That night, my husband came home.

We cooked dinner, washed dishes, put our kids to bed, and went to bed ourselves. I kept thinking of the spouses of those who died who were going to bed alone that night—and every night. I thought of those who would never have the chance to marry and raise families.

In the darkness of our bedroom, I recalled the words of Defense Secretary Cohen from earlier that day. "No one should ever pass an American in uniform without saying, 'Thank you. We're grateful.'"

I suddenly realized why I felt compelled to be at the memorial service. And I told my husband why: "I went for you. I wanted you to know that I don't take what you do lightly. I didn't want you to think that I don't respect and appreciate the risks you've taken. I wanted to go to honor *you*."

5
Having Fun

And if the people find you can fiddle,
Why, fiddle you must, for all your life.
"Fiddler Jones"
Edgar Lee Masters

Navy Social Life

Certainly navy social life has changed a great deal over the past two decades. In the 1970s, and in the history of the navy, there was a great deal of emphasis on the social side of navy life, particularly where navy spouses were involved. To some degree, a sailor's career in earlier times could have been influenced by the social skills and entertainment abilities of the spouse. And during those years there was a rigid separation between officers, chief petty officers, and enlisted sailors in the social setting.

How times have changed.

First, with the explosion in the number of working spouses, many of whom have important careers and jobs of their own, there is far less tendency to have deep spousal involvement in the sailor's navy career. It is now a violation of evaluation guidelines to make even the slightest reference to the sailor's spouse in an evaluation or officer fitness report, although this was quite common before the 1970s. In fact, at the time, a typical comment in a fitness report for a junior officer might be, "Lieutenant Smith's wife Cindy is a perfect navy wife, and the two of them are wonderful assets in the USS *Forrestal*'s wardroom" or, "Together, Lieutenant Commander and Mrs. DiRita are a wonderful navy team." In today's environment, such comments would not be permitted.

Second, there is today very little "command pressure" on spouses to attend functions, participate in fund-raisers, or conduct volunteer work at MCRS or any other organization supporting the navy mission—the navy recognizes that people lead busy and separate lives and are not always able to devote themselves as a couple to the navy. But in the past, such activity was essentially a given of being a navy spouse—the wives (and they typically *were* wives in those days) were expected to attend navy wives club meetings regularly. Of note, there were both officer's wives and enlisted wives clubs, which were rigidly separated. Club members were expected to volunteer in a variety of activities, such as running the base thrift shop. And attendance at the annual navy ball (a fundraising event) was expected of every married couple in the command, as was making appearances at a wide variety of wardroom parties. Today, of course, the "mandatory fun" approach is no longer in effect.

While there is still a wide variety of wonderful social events open to everyone in the Navy—which will be discussed in depth below—there is very little remaining tendency to make them mandatory through subtle career pressure.

Third, the rigid separation between officer, chief petty officer, and enlisted spouses that existed through the first two hundred years of navy life has been relaxed to a large degree socially. Today it is common—indeed, normal—for navy commands to have large social gatherings with everyone, from the youngest sailor to the senior command officer and their entire families invited. A typical destroyer, for example, will have a somewhat formal holiday party at the end of the year, an informal spring picnic and barbecue, and a summer event (perhaps a day at an amusement park, sporting event, or the beach), and they will be "all hands" events, meaning everyone is invited. There may be additional separate parties revolving around the officers, chiefs, first class petty officers, or individual divisions or departments, but the major events of the command are almost always "all hands" oriented.

Additionally, out in the fleet, the old "officer's wives clubs" are a part of history. The current organization is normally called a support group, such as the USS *Nimitz* Family Support Group or the Friends and Families of USS *Barry*. (We will discuss support groups in more detail later.) As the names imply, they are a far cry from the wives clubs of the past; they are open to everyone associated with the command, including spouses, children, friends, family members, and so forth. They can be very lively groups indeed, and they provide a support network, particularly when the ship is deployed.

Overall, the navy's approach to the social side is far broader than it once was. Navy social life now encompasses a wide variety of events, organizations, and philosophies designed to ensure that all navy spouses can find their social niche, should they be interested.

Why You Should *Get Involved*

Although you are not *required* to be the president of your ship's support group (or even be involved), let's discuss why you might *want* to get involved and have fun as part of the many activities available.

There are many great reasons to be involved in your navy.

First, and most important, if your spouse is attached to a seagoing command, you will find yourself alone at home for about half of the evenings your sailor is part of the ship, submarine, or aircraft squadron. During his or her underway periods, and especially during the inevitable six-month deployments, you will want to find and spend time with others in the same situation. The spouses assigned to your command will be the only people who understand and can empathize fully with the challenges of life without your sailor. You can benefit from that kind of support in countless ways, from emergency baby-sitting to simple conversation, and it can become the means for getting through the tough times that are part of a sea tour in today's demanding navy environment.

Second, getting involved is *fun*. For example, a day at an amusement park (Disneyland on the West Coast, or Busch Gardens on the East, perhaps) with the families of your sailor's ship can be a wonderful way to unwind and enjoy yourself with others on the same schedule. Generally such events are reasonably priced and partially subsidized through the command's welfare and recreation committee, and you will undoubtedly find yourself enjoying every minute. Likewise, a well-organized ship's holiday party can be a perfect evening full of good food, dancing, photographs, and perhaps a few meaningful remarks by the ship's captain—truly a memorable time. Even a simple Thanksgiving potluck while the ship is under way can become a very moving event among families missing their sailors but enjoying themselves in good fellowship with friends.

Last, being involved in navy social activities can be an important way to contribute to your nation and community by taking part in good deeds. Virtually every command in the navy sponsors some type of community service, which can be a rewarding experience. Service can range from helping in a food bank or homeless shelter to participating in a recycling project. Additionally, many commands are involved in service activities focused on the navy family itself, giving spouses the opportunity to volunteer at the NMCRS or in an on-base thrift shop. You may feel that as a navy spouse you are already giving a great deal to your nation by sacrificing your sailor as he or she goes away for up to six months at a time—and of course you are right. And sometimes you might feel that, in a busy life, there simply is no time to volunteer; on the other hand, you might be surprised at how good taking part in such activities can make you feel. Do what feels right for you, and if you can find the time for some volunteer work, you *will* feel good about it.

Social Events

Every command has a slightly different approach to throwing parties and conducting social events, but in general all will have a few basic elements. Remember to be pleasant and polite when meeting your spouse's coworkers, and bear in mind that it is customary to address the CO as "Captain." Many COs today will immediately tell spouses—who, after all, don't work for the navy—to call them by their first names. In this regard, you should do what is comfortable for you and what the CO prefers. In general, you cannot go wrong by at least initially taking a formal approach.

With that, here are the most common types of social occasions, with a few thoughts about dress, behavior, and social etiquette at each.

Holiday Party

Almost every navy command will sponsor an end-of-year holiday party. This is an opportunity for the command to use some of the money that has accumulated in the Morale, Welfare, and Recreation (MWR) funds (from the ship's store, soda machines, navy exchanges, etc.) to subsidize a gathering. This is usually a dressy event, with your sailor attending in dress uniform and spouses in formal evening wear. For wives, this can range from an elegant black cocktail dress, perhaps worn with pearls, to a formal evening gown. For husbands, a tuxedo or dark business suit is appropriate.

As with any social function, be careful not to drink too much; and if the party is held at a hotel, as is often the case, consider getting a room and spending the night there. Your command may organize a photographer and flowers for the spouses—if so, take advantage of both. If no flowers are provided, corsages or boutonnieres are appropriate as desired.

Make an effort to meet many people in the command. Now is your opportunity to meet the fellow sailors your spouse talks about. Don't worry about who is senior or junior to your spouse—just get out and mingle.

Spring Picnic

Most commands will hold some kind of spring event, generally an informal type of occasion. A picnic (perhaps a potluck), catered barbecue, or cookout put on by the ship are all possibilities. Casual wear is correct, but avoid anything too revealing or "over the top." Shorts, a nice top, and sandals for wives and casual athletic attire for husbands are appropriate. Come ready for a workout (softball, volleyball, horseshoes, and touch football are typical) and with a good appetite. The children will enjoy this one.

Amusement Park or Sporting Event

Most commands will sponsor a day at a theme park or a sporting event. The most common parks are Seaworld, Disneyland, and Knott's Berry Farm on the West Coast; and Busch Gardens in Williamsburg, Water Country USA, and Paramount's King's Dominion on the East Coast. The sporting events commonly involve baseball, particularly the smaller minor league parks in Norfolk or Jacksonville on the East Coast, or the major league's San Diego Padres on the West Coast. The cost will be subsidized by the command, and sometimes a picnic will be arranged either before or after the game. Wear casual clothes, of course, for either event, and comfortable shoes for the amusement park.

Dining Out

A dining out is a dinner that hearkens back to the earliest days of the service and is often filled with tradition. First, you should be aware of the similarly named events referred to as "mess night" or "dining in." Only service members attend these formal dinners, and they wear their dress uniforms. The events come complete with toasts, a president of the mess, a vice president of the mess, and other ceremonies. Since only service members may attend these events, you (the spouse) would not attend unless you are also in the military.

A dining out, on the other hand, is simply a mess night or dining in to which spouses and dates are invited with the service members. They are dressy affairs, with your spouse in his or her finest dinner dress uniform, so you should be suitably attired. You may want to review the rules of the mess night, which are provided in advance by the command. Simply put, one may not address the mess without permission of the vice president ("Mr. Vice"), and one should observe the rules of the mess (don't be caught with an uncharged [empty] glass when toasts are proposed, rise during toasts, don't depart the table without permission, etc.). These dinners are steeped in tradition and are a treat to attend.

Receptions

A reception is a large party generally given in honor of a dignitary, lasting an hour or two and often featuring a receiving line. If there is a receiving line, there should be an aide to whom you provide your names. As you meet the honoree, you generally confine yourself to a single polite remark, although if no one is in line behind you (an unlikely event) some short conversation is fine. Don't bring food, drink, or cigarettes into a receiving line, and men should wear a coat and tie and women nice dresses.

Navy Birthday Ball

Often referred to simply as the "navy ball," this is often the most formal event of the social year at a naval base or station. It is traditionally held on the weekend closest to 13 October, celebrating the navy's original birthday in 1775. Your sailor will wear a dinner dress uniform, so this is a good opportunity for you to "dress to the nines." Try to "put a table together"—that is, arrange seating with some of your closest navy friends—and consider inviting a civilian couple so they can see what a formal evening with the navy is like.

Calls

All right . . . so almost no one does calls anymore. However, it is still a nice formal custom, so here are the basics:

In the past, officers were expected to call (pay a short social visit, usually receiving light refreshments) on their COs and spouses in their homes; those calls would then be returned by a visit from the CO and spouse (usually a wife) to the junior officer's home. This custom has essentially vanished, and the current custom within navy wardrooms is to have a series of wardroom parties that function as "hails and farewells" (honoring departing officers and meeting newcomers), "wetting downs" (promotion parties), and general events.

Calling Cards

Calling cards were a formal part of the old custom of calls, so they, too, are not seen much anymore in navy social life. Many working spouses today, of course, have business cards, and these can be used as substitutes for the old calling cards if desired. If your host or hostess wants guests to leave calling cards, there should be a tray near the front door. Don't hunt around for it, but if you do see one and if you have cards, feel free to leave one.

If you want purely social calling cards, they should be printed on heavy white or ivory paper in a standard size (three and one-quarter inch by two and one-quarter inch) in a clear font. You should have only your married name printed on the card, for example, Mrs. John Jones.

When paying a call—if you ever do one formally—your spouse would leave one card for the service member and one for the spouse, as well as one for each lady in the house over the age of eighteen. You would leave one card for each lady in the house over the age of eighteen. However, no one leaves more than three cards.

Is this starting to sound a bit "old navy"? Don't worry. You will find very few houses that place a tray out for calling cards; it seems no one expects them anymore. But if you want to participate in this old custom, feel free—it will always be graciously welcomed.

Thank You Notes

An old custom, but one that should *always be honored,* is the sending of a thank you note to the host or hostess after attending *any* social event. It should be mailed within a day or two of the event and need not be more than two or three sentences long. Tell the host or hostess "thank you" and compliment him or her on the event, food, and company. The type of stationery is not important—any nice note-size card is fine. In addition, a nice touch would be to call the day after and give your thanks over the telephone—but this should never be a substitute for a handwritten note.

Write thank you notes—it is a nice custom that we should always keep.

Family Support Group

Over the past ten years, the older idea of a "wives club" has been largely replaced by the family support group. These broad-based organizations are generally open to anyone with a connection to the command and are attended by spouses at all levels, from the most junior's to the CO's. They meet, on average, once a quarter or about every three months. Some of the family support groups will meet more often during deployments—up to once a month.

The meetings vary in their style and intent. Most of them are informational and start with an organizational segment in which the elected board members brief the membership on upcoming events and any items of business. This is followed by a presentation of some type, perhaps a brief on the upcoming schedule by the command, or a discussion of personal safety during deployments, or an overview of programs and services offered by the local NFSC. Refreshments are usually served (brought by volunteers on a rotating basis), and baby-sitting is often available on site.

The real function of the support groups, of course, is simply to get the members of the command's extended family together for fellowship, mutual support, and organization. Information can be passed around, and good deeds (emergency baby-sitting pools, canned goods drives) and preparations for upcoming command social events can be organized.

Family support groups often take a leading role in organizing command-wide parties or social events, or in putting together a homecoming celebration when the command returns from a forward deployment.

During deployments, family support groups often will plan an evening out for the spouses' enjoyment, perhaps at the halfway point in the deployment. These events should be planned with the interests of all spouses in mind so that everyone feels comfortable and included. The groups also work to ensure that all the families are kept up-to-date on the command's status during the deployment, using both the monthly/quarterly meetings and the command's telephone tree. Some family support groups even publish an informal newsletter to keep spouses and their families informed. The command can give the group guidelines on this.

Unfortunately, family support groups can occasionally be sleepy, disorganized, or rumor-and-gossip sessions. Obviously, this is counterproductive to the healthy atmosphere the command would like these groups to engender. If you find this to be the case, discuss the situation honestly and calmly with the command ombudsman or command master chief. They will be interested in your perspective and may ask you to become more involved. Ideally, however, you will not often encounter these problems because in general navy family support groups are very positive, upbeat organizations filled with navy spouses and others interested in fellowship and mutual support. If you enjoy the atmosphere, they can be very beneficial in your role as a sailor's spouse.

Ideas for the Support Group during Deployment

During long deployments, the support group will be looking for ways to get together and keep people feeling connected. An easy way to join a support group is to suggest an activity to the ombudsman or to the support group's leadership. They will be happy to hear from you and may ask your assistance to help organize it. Following are ideas you might want to recommend:

• Secret Pals. Create a questionnaire to be completed by each spouse who would like to participate. Obtain information such as birthday, anniversary date, children's names and birthdays, likes and dislikes, and so on. Gather the questionnaires and have each spouse draw from the pile to become the secret pal to the individual they've chosen. Secret pals send a letter or card on special days, drop off a gift, and become acquainted with another spouse in the command.

• Wok Party. Ask each spouse to bring a presliced ingredient for a large stir-fry. Have several woks cooking—beef, chicken, vegetarian—

and make up a big pot of steamed rice. Get oriental beer and see who is willing to use the chopsticks.

• Celebrity Party. Consider a variation for your Halloween party and have everyone dress as their favorite celebrity. You can have prizes for the most creative, closest in appearance, and most difficult to identify. Ask attendees to bring the beverage their celebrity would most likely drink.

• Healthy Outing. Try an event that focuses on fitness; perhaps a long walk along a trail or a day at the base gym. Most base gyms would be happy to provide a group trainer and offer professional advice on machine use and exercise programs.

• Wedding Album Shower. Request that everyone bring their wedding photos. Consider serving a homemade wedding cake, complete with a miniature bride and groom on the top. Bring out the photos and award a prize for the longest married, the shortest wedding dress, or the widest lapels on the groom's tuxedo. A few brave spouses might even squeeze into their wedding outfits!

• Ethnic Cooking Demonstration. Ask spouses from a certain culture—Italian, Greek, Philippine—to do a cooking demonstration. Serve an appropriate wine or other beverage and let everyone pitch in and help.

• Baby Picture Night. Request everyone to bring pictures of their babies and their deployed spouse. Present prizes for the person who can match the most babies and spouses, the cutest outfit, the funniest expression, and so on.

• Kids' Costume Party. Consider having the kids dress up for St. Valentine's Day, the Fourth of July, Thanksgiving, the Oscars, or any other event.

• St. Patrick's Day Party. Decorate your surroundings in green and involve the children by having them dress like leprechauns. Serve lots of green cookies and search for gold foil-covered chocolate coins.

• Baskets for the Sailors Night. Encourage everyone to bring treats that can be mixed and matched, and sent to the deployed sailors. Use shoe boxes to fill and to mail, and make sure the kids are included.

Entertaining

As a navy spouse, you may find yourself able to undertake some entertaining in your home. This can vary depending on your sailor's position within the command, from the fairly frequent requirements facing senior officers to the casual opportunities that can be an enjoyable part of a junior enlisted spouse's role in the navy.

In general, the point of good entertaining is to make people feel comfortable and happy. Don't try to impress anyone or worry too much about putting together complicated dinners or parties. Organization and advance planning are the keys to success, and you should be able to find many helpful books in the local library with ideas for entertaining. Experiment with new dishes and ideas on your family and closest friends first, and always keep your sense of humor. Don't hesitate to invite more senior couples—they will appreciate your thoughtfulness in including them.

What follows are some entertaining pointers and a few common situations, with suggestions for easy execution.

Invitations

The first step in planning any event is to send out the invitations. Be sure you get them out early, and include "RSVP" on the bottom of the card, letter, or printed invitation, along with your telephone number. Shortly after you send them out, you should receive telephone calls accepting (or regretfully declining) your invitation. Or you may opt to use the expression "regrets only" so that only those who cannot attend need call you.

If you are the recipient of an invitation with an RSVP, call the host or hostess as soon as you can to let them know your plans. Remember, it is very rude simply to ignore an invitation.

Wardroom Parties

At some point, most officers' spouses will be involved in a wardroom party for the officers in the command. These are generally casual cocktail parties, although occasionally dinner parties are organized. If you are involved in one, first check with the wardroom mess treasurer to see if there is any support normally provided. Some command wardrooms organize a so-called "liquor locker," a store of various cocktails, wine, and beer that is mutually purchased with the wardroom mess share and that is then available to use at parties. Additionally, some wardrooms will have willing younger officers (generally the unmarried ensigns) pitch in and help set up for an affair.

The best approach is to serve some light hors d'oeuvres, set up a couple of ice chests with various bottled beers, organize a wine bar, and ensure that plenty of sodas and alternatives to liquor are available. One way to make such a gathering more interesting is to throw it in associ-

This happy couple is enjoying a wardroom party. Author's collection.

ation with another command-sponsored function—for example, you could provide a brief round of cocktails before the annual holiday party or have dessert, coffee, and brandy after a dinner out with wardroom members and spouses.

Wardroom parties often are set up to welcome new arrivals to a wardroom and honor departees, hence the name "hails and farewells." If this is the case, work with the XO of the command to ensure that all presentation items (e.g., plaques, gifts, flowers) are on station when the CO is ready to say a few words about the honorees. The XO generally will make sure that the items are handed to the CO at the appropriate time.

Be careful and observant as to consumption of alcohol, and ensure that anyone who has overindulged is offered alternative transportation. Be insistent no matter who the culprit is. If need be, enlist the assistance of the CO or XO to corral anyone who is uncooperative.

Wetting Down Celebrations

An old navy tradition that you will become involved in is "wetting down" a new rank. Whenever your sailor is promoted, there is an opportunity to put on a small party to celebrate his or her new status in the navy. The event can range from a few friends at the house for beer, chips, and salsa during a basketball game, to very large and elaborate outings, generally staged by several newly promoted individuals who together put on an open bar and substantial food at an on-base club.

The key to the wetting down ceremony is moderation. In the past, they have tended to get a little out of hand, with the natural exuberance of the moment flowing over into an overindulgence in alcohol. If you are involved in setting up a wetting down celebration, make sure excessive drinking is discouraged, alternative beverages are offered, and transportation home is provided for those who are inebriated.

The old tradition was to spend the difference in three months' pay on a wetting down, but in today's navy that is generally too much. A better solution is to have a modest cocktail party at home, perhaps combining it with "hails and farewells" for some members of the command; or have your sailor take his friends by the club or a bar on the way home for a round of drinks on him or her. Another less expensive and more reasonable approach is to get together with others promoted at the same time (e.g., all of the new chief petty officers) and put on an affair for the rest of the appropriate group. This keeps the cost down and ensures everyone is part of the event.

Division Parties

Most commands are organized around divisions, which can range in size from small groups of less than a dozen sailors to large organizations with fifty or more. The type of party therefore must be tailored to the size and seniority of the organization, but a safe bet is to work it around the viewing of a sports event of some kind—a football or basketball game will provide a rallying point for some of the more reserved sailors, and such events are always popular. Alternatively, a barbecue or bowling night is fun and can be a relaxing setting for many sailors and their spouses, and an ice cream social can be entertaining and fairly simple to set up.

Check with the division officer regarding the availability of MWR funds. Generally, each quarter every division in the command can receive a nominal amount of money to sponsor a divisional party. The funds either can be allowed to accumulate for an annual event or taken each quarter for a smaller type of social gathering.

As always, make sure alternative beverages are available, and very carefully watch for and don't allow underage drinking. Have a designated driver available, and be sure the leading chief petty officer or petty officer is ready to help out if anyone becomes difficult.

Potluck Supper

A popular activity for a family support group or any smaller group of spouses (a divisional spouse's party or a wardroom spouse's gathering, for example), the potluck supper is easy to organize. The key is to make sure the basics are covered, with someone assigned for each of the major components: salads, main courses, beverages, desserts. You will be surprised at the wonderfully inventive dishes people bring. An alternative is to ask everyone to bring their favorite appetizer, salad, or dessert, then just order pizza or Chinese food for a main course, with everyone chipping in to cover the cost. Use disposable plates (but perhaps something a little nicer than plain paper), and let everyone pitch in for cleanup. If children are coming, try to set up a play area for them, and have some videos on hand to keep them occupied after they have had a chance to run around and eat. And of course make sure nonalcoholic beverages are available, watch closely for any sign of excessive drinking, and designate drivers if needed.

Never hesitate to invite people to an event because your house is small or because you feel you don't have the necessary supplies and equipment with which to entertain. Guests will not expect fine china and Waterford crystal. They are happy to be invited and always anxious to pitch in to help, no matter what your situation. If you think you would enjoy entertaining, do it, and be creative.

A Few Good Rules about Entertaining

- Relax, no one expects you to find a cure for cancer. You are just cooking dinner, and people are always delighted just being asked.

- Do not try a new dish on anyone outside of your family.

- Most people love pasta, Mexican food, or anything cooked on a grill.

- Plan ahead and write down the ingredients before you go shopping.

- Do not overfill your guests with heavy appetizers.

- Make more food than you think you will need.

- Create fresh green salads and small, simple desserts.

- Always have beer, wine, and sodas. Anything else is optional.

- In addition to coffee, offer sparkling water with dessert.

- Clean up as you go.

- Let husbands and wives sit next to each other—we spend enough time apart in the navy.

- No matter what happens, keep your sense of humor and laugh frequently.

Visiting the Ship

Coming down to your sailor's ship or submarine is a fun event and may be something you do fairly frequently—especially if he or she is "on duty" (i.e., spending the night on board every five days or so). You can come down during the evening hours and enjoy dinner on board with your spouse, and even stay to watch a movie or spend some time together. Don't be a stranger to your spouse's command—you will find the time very enjoyable.

Wives should wear slacks and low-heeled shoes to visit a ship, unless there is a formal ceremony requiring a dress. Short shorts, halter tops, flip-flops, and very casual attire are not appropriate and should be avoided. Wives also should bring purses with shoulder straps, since both hands need to be free on occasion to move about safely.

When coming aboard, you will need to cross a brow. Be careful, use the handrails, and move only as fast as you want to. When you are at the top of the brow, just before coming aboard, it is customary to turn momentarily and face the American flag. This will be on the stern (back part) of the ship—a good way to determine the location is to watch the person ahead of you. If your sailor is ahead of you, he or she will turn in the correct direction and—if in uniform—salute the flag. Facing the flag is a sign of respect.

If you plan on visiting, be on time. Your spouse will not appreciate waiting around the quarterdeck (entrance to the ship) for you, since it is a busy and ceremonial place. You should plan on leaving at 10:00 P.M. (taps) at the very latest, and you may never roam about the ship unescorted.

If you are a frequent visitor to the ship, it would be a nice practice to invite some of your spouse's shipmates over to your home on occasion. Another nice touch is occasionally to bring a box of freshly baked cookies for his or her shipmates and leave them in the wardroom or chief's mess, or on the mess decks.

Friends and Family Cruises

While navy ships will never rival Carnival Cruise Lines, your command may organize a cruise that permits friends and family to come to sea. These have been called dependents' cruises in the past, although more recently they are referred to as "friends and family cruises." This is an opportunity not to be missed.

The day will start early, with a 9:00 A.M. underway time from the local naval station. Be sure to wear comfortable clothes, and by all means bring the children, as long as they are over the required age for the cruise (usually eight years old). The ship will go to sea and demonstrate a variety of activities, all designed to show you what your sailor is doing out at sea all that time. You may see the ship's guns fire, take tours of the engineering plant, enjoy a delicious meal or barbecue, operate the ship's fire-fighting equipment, watch flight operations, see the berthing compartments, or do any of a number of other things with your sailor.

Remember that, despite the presence of many friends and families, the ship must still be operated in a safe and professional manner. Respect the boundaries that are set up, and be quiet and self-contained in operating stations like the bridge and the combat information center. Always supervise your children and keep them under control—don't permit them to "run wild" throughout the ship. Going to sea is a dangerous activity, but it can be delightful, especially when you get to return at the end of the day and head home.

Family support groups may be involved in some aspect of the friends and family cruises; if so, and if you are part of a group, be sure to pitch in and help out. Members may hand out name tags, organize tours, or do some recruiting and publicizing for the organization. Be involved.

Change of Command

One of the premier social events in the navy is the time-honored change of command ceremony. It marks the day when one officer surrenders command of a navy unit (e.g., ship, submarine, squadron, shore base) to another officer. The historical precedents of the change of command ceremony date to the ancient Greeks, who held such events when passing command of individual vessels at sea.

During the early years of the navy, the change of command ceremony was actually very short. The outgoing officer merely introduced the relieving officer to the crew, followed by the reading of orders by the incoming captain. The new captain might (or might not) choose to make a few remarks about his approach to command. Everyone would then go about their business, with perhaps an extra portion of rum or an extra serving of plum duff (a popular dessert in the nineteenth century) being served later in the day. A brief ceremony, with no invited guests and little ceremonial activity, remained the norm throughout the better part of the twentieth century.

In recent years, however, the change of command ceremony has evolved into a somewhat longer (about an hour) event, usually followed by a reception of some sort. It has shifted from a purely military occasion to one with distinct social overtones, and one to which you may be invited many times over the course of your spouse's navy career.

Today, change of command ceremonies include formal invitations, elaborate bunting and decoration, a band, formal programs, speeches by an invited guest speaker and the outgoing and incoming COs, an invocation by a chaplain, presentation of a commissioning pennant to the outgoing CO, and an extensive reception, generally with a buffet and open bar.

The spouses associated with the command are generally all invited, although you will probably not receive a formal invitation. Invitations to families are simply issued through the ship. Don't hesitate to attend, as these ceremonies are interesting and often a good setting to socialize with other members of the command.

Dress is normally formal, with sailors in service dress uniforms and spouses in corresponding attire. A nice dress or suit for wives and a dark business suit for husbands are appropriate. Go through the receiving line if one is set up; if not, make sure you thank both the incoming and outgoing COs for inviting you. The food and drink are provided at their personal expense, so thanks are entirely appropriate. You may also want to say something pleasant to the outgoing CO, such as, "We'll certainly miss you on the ship," or words to that effect. And it is just as appropriate to mention to the new captain what a great command it is and to offer congratulations. The two officers will welcome your remarks.

Children are usually welcome at a change of command, although they should be about eight years or older. Exceptions are made for the children of the incoming or outgoing COs, of course. If you have any questions about any aspect of the change of command, call the ship's ombudsman, or have your sailor raise them on the ship with the XO or through the chain of command.

Retirement

The retirement ceremony (a very special occasion), marks the end of at least twenty years of individual service. The ceremony may be held in an office, on a ship, at a park, or in any other location chosen by the retiree. It generally lasts about thirty minutes and will include a speaker, the presentation of a medal and flag to the retiree, and a few words about the retiree's spouse as well.

You should be honored to be invited to a retirement ceremony, and a reception usually follows. Attire is relatively formal, as befits a serious and meaningful ceremony.

What to Wear

A few thoughts on attire when attending ceremonies:

Very Formal

The invitation will be for an evening event, after 6:00 P.M., and will specify "white tie" on the invitation. Such an event is almost never seen, except in the case of retiring senior flag officers and military officers involved in diplomatic corps functions. For wives, very formal evening gowns are appropriate; husbands should wear a tuxedo with tails and a white tie. You will not attend a lot of these.

Formal

These events also are held after 6:00 P.M., and the invitation will specify "black tie." An example would be a navy ball or a civilian-equivalent dinner dance. Wives should wear evening gowns, husbands a tuxedo or dinner jacket.

Informal

Don't be fooled by these words on an invitation. "Informal" differs from "casual." Informal attire means coats and ties for husbands, and for wives nice afternoon dresses or suits during daytime events and evening dresses after dark.

Casual

This can vary widely, but generally a casual event means a collared shirt and nice slacks for men, with a sport coat (never a tie); and for ladies, slacks and a blouse, or nice shorts. Jeans, T-shirts, beach clothes, sports gear, and so forth should not be worn unless the host or hostess specifically indicates they are appropriate or the event clearly requires them (a ship's picnic at the beach, or a softball outing, for example).

Military Courtesy

Despite the growing realization within the military that spouses have their own place in the world and are not in any way part of the military rank or rate structure, it is still worthwhile to have a firm understanding of the basics of military courtesy.

The military is hierarchical, with uniforms and markings indicating where everyone stands at all times. While this may seem anachronistic to civilians in this day and age, such a structure is necessary because of the unique character of the military's task: to enter the violent world of combat, where instant obedience to orders is an absolute requirement to ensure the safety of all in the unit. There is no time in war or in the emergencies of peacetime training to sort out position and obligation— they must be second nature to everyone.

Consequently, even in social settings there tends to be a fairly set structure to the relations between individuals. In other words, even though your sailor takes off his uniform at night, he or she is still bound to the social and hierarchical conventions it represents, even when far from the unit. A prime example is the command party. Even out on the softball field at the ship's picnic, or on the floor dancing at the squadron's Christmas party, the conventions of address and respect pertain. Your sailor will still refer to those more senior by their appropriate rank and with respect.

You, as a navy spouse, are in a different position, although common sense and general courtesy always apply. A good approach is initially to take a formal tone, and often the older or more senior individual will ask you to call him or her by first name. Remember that the CO, on first introduction, is referred to as "Captain." Once the CO invites you to refer to him or her by a first name (and COs usually do these days), feel free to do so, if you are comfortable with the practice. The same rule holds true for anyone else in the unit. The exception, of course, is if you—the spouse—are also a member of the service; in that case, the normal military courtesies apply, and you would refer to the individual by rank and with the appropriate "sir" or "ma'am." Your children, of course, should be taught to refer to adults by their rank and title, just as they would to any other older individual.

Another issue of military courtesy deals with public displays of affection. There is dignity in the navy profession, and it should be respected in this regard. While a light kiss, a hug hello or good-bye, and holding hands while walking down the pier are acceptable, refrain from more serious physical contact until you are in a private setting. This can be difficult when your sailor is about to set off on a long cruise, so the best solution is to say your farewells in the privacy of your home and let the pier-side departure be one of dignity and respect for the challenges ahead.

Parades

Once a frequent occurrence in the navy, the number of parades has declined in recent years. They are now uncommon enough that everyone should seize the opportunity to view a parade. You can see them at the U.S. Naval Academy in Annapolis, Maryland, during the fall and spring, and at the navy boot camps in Orlando, Florida; San Diego, California; and Great Lakes, Illinois. Parades usually are held on Fridays, but call any of the aforementioned commands to obtain their schedules. Marine Corps bases also occasionally hold parades.

Parades are for the most part held during fair weather and are normally attended in relatively conservative attire. Spring or summer parades are perfect opportunities to show off a beautiful summer frock or a tropical suit. If you are lucky enough to be invited to VIP seating, you will be under an awning; if not, a straw hat is appropriate and adds a touch of dash to the event. Go out for gin and tonics (or whatever beverage you enjoy) after the parade.

Divine Worship

In the "old navy" one would see everyone from the base turn out for chapel on Sundays; the small services held on the ships were well attended also. Parents scrubbed the children, and families often would head over to the club for brunch when services were over. Going to chapel was, in every sense, a social event.

Today it has changed. In fact, divine worship at navy facilities, both ashore and afloat, generally is not heavily attended. And it certainly has lost any character of social interaction at most navy bases. Yet it still is touched by the tradition of the military service, and it is well worth checking into as a navy spouse. You may find real solace in the church, especially during difficult and challenging times such as prolonged deployments. Navy chaplains are always ready to help, and they understand the unique life of the navy spouse. Additionally, many of the beautiful old chapels are wonderful places to worship and refresh oneself spiritually—notably the U.S. Naval Academy chapel in Annapolis, arguably the most beautiful structure in the entire service and well worth a visit if you are in the area.

Your new arrival can be christened on your spouse's ship. Author's collection.

You may also be pleasantly surprised by the spirit and enthusiasm at divine worship services held on board ship. And don't forget, if you give birth while your spouse is attached to the ship, the new arrival can be christened on the ship, in the ship's bell, by a navy chaplain. Your child's name then will be inscribed in the bell with the date of the christening, thereby linking you forever to the ship. Give navy divine worship a chance—as a navy spouse, you may find it fits your life very well. And the brunches at the club aren't bad, either.

Deployment Fun

Yes, I admit it—deployments are *not* fun. So why discuss them in this chapter? Because even though the overall situation—suddenly being alone, with your sailor so far away—is not fun, you should be able to come up with some enjoyable activities. If you are unable to think of them as "fun" during a deployment, call them mental health breaks or "what I do to keep my sanity while my sailor is gone"; the point is, there is much you can do during a deployment—with yourself, other navy spouses, or your children—that is quite enjoyable. The following are a few ideas.

On Your Own

• Further your education. Take a foreign language class, work on your degree, study history or literature. Open your mind.

• Find employment or advance your standing in your profession. Take advantage of employer-sponsored training programs or other opportunities. Talk to the personnel officer where you work. If you don't work, consider a full-time or part-time job.

• Volunteer to help others. Work in a nursing home, at your local Fisher House, or tutor disadvantaged children. Become a big brother or sister. There is much need throughout our nation for volunteers.

• Learn a new craft. Paint, sculpt, make pottery (inexpensive and expressive).

• Exercise. Get in shape. Explore opportunities on base. It will be easier if you go with a friend.

• Read. Go to the library. Magazines, books, pamphlets—there is much to read and learn.

• Join a church. Explore the spiritual side of life. Learn about your religion. Get involved in a study group focusing on the Bible, Talmud, or Koran as your faith requires.

• Focus more on your children, their needs, and their growth.

• Travel. Go to a port where your sailor has pulled in for several days. Or simply take day trips in the area. Go to the closest national park for a hike, a lecture on nature, a history talk. Visit the museums in your area.

With Your Command's Support Group

• Have a group dinner at an ethnic restaurant—generally expensive and adventurous.

• Go bowling. So what if you are terrible? Bowling alleys are fun group activity centers, and they are inexpensive for the time involved.

• Take a tour of another navy activity in the area, or a museum.

• Invite a guest speaker to your group to give a talk on books, history or art, or on something more practical, such as emergency auto repair, home security, or job hunting.

• Have a grooming workshop, with a representative from a cosmetic company.

- Learn a craft, with someone in your group taking the lead in teaching others.

- Have a wine-tasting party, with someone knowledgeable to guide your group through the basics of reds, whites, and blushes.

- Play cards, and perhaps teach a new game to the group—bridge is coming back.

- Potlucks are fun. Pick an ethnic night, and have a designated "chef" who shows the group how to cook Chinese, Italian, Mexican, and so forth. Or have a "my spouse's favorite" night, and take plenty of pictures for your sailors.

- Have a slumber party. Rent videos, make popcorn, tell stories.

- Hold a "build a sub" night, with everyone bringing something to add to the sandwiches. Get good-quality bread.

- Visit a nursing home, VA hospital, or children's hospital ward. Bring baskets of goodies.

- Prepare holiday baskets for the needy, especially at Thanksgiving and Christmas.

- Adopt a shelter, cause, or family. Take care of them and be involved.

- Focus on an elementary school. Tutor the young children, put up a bulletin board, go to the assemblies and sporting events. Your sailor's command may already have an adopted school—keep the link alive while the ship is on cruise.

At Home or Out with Your Children

- Hang up a map and show where your sailor is going, letting the children put up tacks and read about the countries Mom or Dad is visiting.

- Plan menus at home that reflect the country being visited. Learn a little about the culture, a few phrases from the language, a song, or the art or music of the region. Tell your sailor about it in a letter from the children.

- Have three time chains with paper links, one representing months (6 links), one weeks (24), and one days (180). As the links come off the chains, mail them to your sailor.

- Get together with all of the children from the command and have an ice cream social and sundae party, with each family bringing their favorite toppings.

A holiday party, with Santa as the guest of honor, on board the USS Barry. *Author's collection.*

• Host a command picnic in the park or at the base pool, with planned events and barbecue grills set up. Make sure someone with a video camera captures the events for your sailors.

• Sponsor theme parties for holidays while the command is deployed, including:

Valentine's Day—Cookie bake and valentine construction, then mail the spoils to your sailor.

Easter—Easter egg hunt is, of course, mandatory. Fill the eggs not only with candy, but coins, gift certificates to local fast-food restaurants, and other small tokens. Have a "golden" egg with a big prize. Have someone dress up as the Easter bunny for photos, and finish it off with a potluck Easter brunch.

Fourth of July—Lends itself to a picnic, but this is also a good time for making a float or a banner to celebrate our nation's birthday. You are demonstrating a great deal of patriotism by supporting your sailor's deployment, so you may as well celebrate it.

Halloween—Your group can put together a haunted house, using different rooms for different themes and levels of "scariness." You can also have a Halloween carnival with traditional fall games. A costume contest is always a hit, along with a children's parade in costume before they go off for trick-or-treating. A nice touch is to have a character, perhaps a "great pumpkin" wandering around dispensing candy.

Christmas or holiday season—Be sensitive to non-Christians' reactions to designated Christmas parties, and consider calling your gatherings "holiday" parties. Some ideas include gifts from Santa, carnival games, taking everyone to a holiday show, going caroling, making ornaments, having a holiday movie night (with popcorn and movies), making Christmas or holiday cards, and filling stockings (for your sailors, the needy in the area, or the children themselves).

In the end, having fun in the navy is all about attitude. If you keep your spirits up, take reasonable opportunities to enjoy yourself, and don't allow yourself to become discouraged by the challenges, you can and will have a wonderful time as a navy spouse.

6
Always Moving

"What shall I say, brave Admiral, say,
If we sight naught but seas at dawn?"
"Why, you shall say at break of day,
Sail on! sail on! and on!"

"Columbus"
Joaquin Miller

When I think about a lifetime of moving with the military, both as a navy junior and a navy wife, I'm reminded of the beginning of *A Tale of Two Cities* by Charles Dickens: "It was the best of times, it was the worst of times."

There are pleasant and difficult aspects to moving every two to three years. The difficulties are obvious: dealing with the occasional careless mover who breaks furniture and loses rugs, sorting out new schools, changing jobs, finding new friends, driving unfamiliar roads, looking for new doctors and dentists—the list goes on and on. It is part of human nature to dislike change.

Yet there are positive aspects to the constant cycle of moving as well. Over the horizon, in that new city, are unexpected pleasures. Better restaurants, perhaps. A nicer, newer house without a loud dog barking half the night living next door. And the sixth-grade teacher may be much better than the one your daughter had in your previous duty assignment. Actual improvements will vary from place to place, of course, but in my experience there are always a handful of things that will be better no matter where you move from or where you are headed.

Finally, there are the intangible benefits of frequent moves. These include the opportunity constantly to refresh your circle of friends, affording you new ideas and ways of approaching life; the excitement and challenge of new surroundings; a sense that something better is just over the horizon; children who generally are more outgoing, friendly, and confident because they have learned to make friends easily; and the confidence that comes from handling new situations easily.

Moving is not easy. But it has its rewards, and if you stay focused on the positive and keep your sense of humor, you will do fine. And despite all of your complaints about moving every two to three years, consider

Saying goodbye to San Diego. Author's collection.

that most people who finally retire after a career of moving about inevitably find themselves "looking for orders" around three years after they have settled into their "dream house."

The Mechanics

Your moving cycle will begin formally the day your spouse comes home and says something like, "Well, I talked to the detailer today, and it looks like we're moving next summer to . . . " This is an exciting moment. After an inward sigh at the prospect of giving up your fifth grader's wonderful violin teacher and the certainty that there will *not* be a good veterinarian in your new location, you look at your spouse and say, "Great." And with that, you begin the process of gathering information about your new homeport, planning to close up shop in your current location, and thinking about the many details involved in your move.

Nothing formal can happen until your spouse receives written orders. You should keep your sailor focused on obtaining orders, and sometimes that means he or she must call the detailer (the representative at the Bureau of Naval Personnel) once or twice. Money for moves and thus for writing orders becomes a little tight at the end of each fiscal year (30 September), so the earlier in the fiscal year you work on orders the better. If the bureau is not forthcoming with orders, and you are supposed to be moving in less than ninety days, have your sailor go to the chain of command at the unit for assistance. You *must* have orders in hand within three months of the move or you may run into trouble setting up packers and movers.

Once you have the papers in hand, pick a day to move out of your house and arrange it with the nearest Personal Property Shipping Office (PPSO) or Personal Property Transportation Office (PPTO). (You may also hear it called the "transportation office" or the "household goods" office.) These offices vary widely in quality and methodology, but the basic drill should be as follows: once you know you are moving, get the PPSO number from the base telephone book or your command ombudsman, then call to see if you can make an appointment over the telephone. You need to work with "outgoing" shipments. As soon as you have orders and can give a move-out date, begin working with the PPSO. This is especially true for early summer moves (June–July), which tend to get booked up quickly. When you visit the PPSO, take your ID card, a dozen copies of your spouse's orders, and a written letter authorizing you to set up the shipment on your sailor's behalf. (Your general power of attorney will also work here.) Failure to have these items will bring the entire process to a halt. This strict procedure is for the protection of the service member.

Ideally, you will be able to get an appointment over the telephone, but some PPSOs will tell you to come in between 8:00 A.M. and 12:00 P.M. Monday, Wednesday, or Friday. If such is the case, try to get a babysitter and bring a book or magazine, because you may wait an hour or more just to see a counselor. On top of that, the process of setting up the move will take about an hour from the moment you sit down with him or her.

Once you are with a counselor, he or she will ask a series of questions, beginning with when you would like to move out of your house. You should be prepared to furnish a date and an alternate, the weight of your total household goods (figure about one thousand pounds per room), any heavy specialty items you need to have moved (the office has a list: pianos, canoes, refrigerators, etc.), and any special requirements (antique furniture that requires special crating, for example). Be aware that the government will not move loaded firearms, loose ammunition, any explosives, propane tanks that are not certified empty (any propane dealer can do this for you), motorcycles, alcohol in open containers (sometimes the movers will tape these shut for you), or live animals. They also will not assume financial responsibility for unique items of personal value (photo albums, paintings with sentimental value, etc.). All of your information will be transferred to several forms. If you have an unusually complicated situation, the counselor may have an agent come to your house and do a walk-around with you to resolve any questions. Then you will be assigned a day or two for the packing of your goods; the next day, the movers will load them on the truck and take them away.

If possible, you should try to set up what is called a "door-to-door" move. This is when you can leave one house and meet the movers several days later at the new one. This may be difficult to do, but it can be accomplished with careful planning. The advantage is that by doing so you will avoid two potentially damaging moves for your furniture (coming off the truck into temporary storage in the new town, and back onto the truck when you have it delivered to the new house). With a door-to-door move you will be there to watch the movers load and unload your belongings at both ends of the move, and therefore won't have nightmares of them manhandling everything while out of your sight—after watching the movers throw things around while you are there, you can imagine how your furniture is handled when you *aren't* there. So go for the door-to-door move if at all possible.

Of course, there are some things you must and/or probably should move yourself: ammunition (if you want to move firearms yourself, have your sailor check with the base police for information, laws, and regulations on moving such items around the country and across state lines); family photo albums and other irreplaceable personal items; cameras; electronics; furs; any items whose value would be difficult to prove, such as small antiques, sterling silver, jewelry, fine art; and alcohol in opened containers (e.g., wines and liquors). If you own a number of valuable antiques or oriental rugs that will be put on the moving truck, you should have these items professionally appraised. Otherwise, if damaged, they will be assessed as ordinary "old furniture" when a damage claim is filed. An appraisal can be a very good investment.

Don't be afraid to ask about special arrangements (e.g., crating for large, valuable antiques), and if you have anything appraised, make it clear to the PPSO that if the government will not crate your antique corner cabinet, for example (which was appraised in writing for $12,000), you will claim for all damage. People at the PPSO generally will work with you. If you are not satisfied with the service you receive, don't hesitate to speak with a supervisor—and if necessary, go up the chain until you speak to a uniformed navy officer. If you still come away unhappy, don't be afraid to have your sailor take it up with the chain of command on the ship as well. Remember, you are the customer and the PPSO is there to serve you, not the other way around.

Even if you do encounter problems, you should try to be a cooperative and friendly consumer at all times. The armed forces execute nearly a million moves each year at a cost of over $3 billion, so the system is very experienced and very busy. The trick is to make sure you receive fair treatment, and to speak up when problems arise to ensure you do. Some other points to consider:

- You can arrange your move through offices run by the other services, but bear in mind that the name might be different: the Installation Transportation Office (army); Traffic Management Office (air force); and Household Goods Shipping Office (coast guard). (The Marine Corps office, like the navy's, is called PPSO.) All offices work for the installation commanders (in the navy, the base CO is ultimately responsible). The number for the overall moving command for the armed forces, which is called the Military Traffic Management Command, is 1-800-756-6862.

- You can ask for a particular shipper. If you have a recommendation or prior experience, this is not a bad idea. Your request may not be honored, but it is worth a try.

- Ask for "containerized shipping," which means everything is put in large crates for shipping. If your goods go into storage, they will remain in these sealed crates, thus preventing excessive handling of your furniture. Crating, or a "code 2," is not always authorized because of the expense, but it is worth asking for one. You may be charged more, but ask for details.

When your goods arrive at your new location, what happens next depends on the arrangements you have made. A door-to-door shipment means you will (ideally) be waiting at your new home when it arrives. If you will not be moving into your new home immediately (the most typical case), your goods will go into temporary, or "temp," storage. Temp storage can last 90 days initially, with an option to apply for another 90 days. Sometimes you can store it for up to 270 days (in 90-day increments), but generally after that you will not be allowed continued storage at government expense. Temp storage may be necessary if you are on the waiting list for government quarters, unable to find a rental quickly, or in the process of buying or building a new home. If your arrangements are simply "up in the air," you can have your goods put into nontemporary storage in certain circumstances, such as an overseas tour in which you will not be taking everything with you.

Remember, *you* are the ultimate quality assurance inspector associated with the move. While the PPSO generally will have an inspector stop by for a ten-minute walk-around during the move, your job is to watch the packers and movers carefully. It is customary to keep a supply of sodas and water in the refrigerator for them, but you are not required to buy them lunch, and tipping is not done. Be friendly but firm, and make sure they understand early that you are on top of the situation, aware of your rights, and very engaged in the packing and moving. You always have the right to stop a move at any point if, for example (these are actual experiences), a mover is drunk, unruly, uncooperative, damaging your goods, or smoking in your home despite warnings. Order them out of the house and immediately call an inspector to adjudicate the situation. With that in mind, you should know your responsibilities in the moving process, as well as the movers'.

You should:

- remove TV antenna

- empty and clean the refrigerator and freezer (tape a prepackaged coffee filter pack inside to prevent smell and mildew during the move)

- drain water from hot tubs or water beds

- remove window air conditioners

- disconnect all electronics (if you have original boxes, repack the items in them), washers, dryers, and other appliances

- dispose of any unwanted items. (you will be glad you did)

- remove pictures and other items from the walls

- dismantle outdoor play equipment into movable pieces

- remove items from attic or storage areas that are not easily accessible

- hose down and clean outdoor furniture, grills, etc., so they go on the truck pest free (this is important, and in many areas of the country you will be asked to sign forms verifying this has been done)

- make a video or shoot photos of your property, with close-ups of any smaller valuable items. (This is an important record to have prior to a move, and it can be valuable in the event of a fire, flood, hurricane, or any other emergency. Store it at your parents' home or in a safe deposit box.)

Naturally, you must be home for both the packing and pickup of your goods. Your primary job is to provide quality assurance to the movers.

But what about the specific duties of the carrier, you may ask. Be aware that they should:

- use new, clean packing materials (no excelsior or newspaper is allowed)

- pack mirrors, pictures, and glass objects in specially designed and protected cartons

- wrap and protect all finished surfaces

- roll and protect rugs

- pack professional books and papers in separate and clearly marked containers (these items will not be included in your weight limit)

- mark each carton to show general contents

- prepare an accurate and legible inventory

- remove all leftover packing material from your residence

Once you have reached your new destination, again, both you and the shipper have specific responsibilities. You need to:

- call the transportation office immediately to let them know how to contact you and to reconfirm your delivery date. (If they cannot reach you, your goods will go into temporary storage. Be sure you are accessible by telephone if you don't want this to happen.)

- provide directions for the placement of furniture (the movers are only required to move it once) when the off-load begins at your new home

- check off each item from the inventory as it enters the house

- list any damaged or missing items on the appropriate form—don't sign for any services not actually performed

The carrier's responsibilities are as follows:

- unpack and unwrap all cartons, boxes, and crates (you can choose to decline this)

- put each item or carton in the room you indicate

- assemble all furniture and equipment disassembled by the movers at origin

- uncover appliances (they are not required to hook them up)

- remove all packing material resulting from unpacking

A big decision at your destination is whether or not to have the movers unpack and unwrap everything. (This is the carriers' responsibility, but an option on your part.) The task can be quite time consuming, with movers still in the house late into the night. If you want them to do the unpacking/unwrapping but don't feel they can finish by day's end, call the company early in the day and request additional personnel. Often, carriers will drag their feet unloading, hoping to pressure the customer into dismissing them and thereby escaping any additional labor. In fact, some customers do prefer to do their own unpacking at their leisure. My advice is to require the movers to unpack kitchen parcels and most boxes, but to leave clothes and books in their cartons until you are ready to unpack them yourself. Otherwise, you may find the clutter of unpacked items overwhelming, thus making settling in even more time consuming. And remember to make sure the movers take all of the used cardboard and wrapping paper. If you have any problems, call the local PPSO for assistance and they will dispatch an inspector. Don't sign a form indicating the movers unpacked your goods if they did not—this is a frequent scam. Make sure they did everything listed in the paperwork. Know your rights and ensure you get what you want. This is *your* move.

Other Moving Issues

Besides the items mentioned earlier, certain other items that cannot be shipped or stored as household goods at government expense include airplanes, automobiles, trucks, vans, campers, farm equipment, cordwood, and building materials. You can ship professional books, tools, papers, specialized clothing, communications equipment used with MARS, field clothing, and uniforms without regard to the weight allowance. While unloaded firearms can be shipped, they must be completely described on the inventory as to make, model, serial number, and caliber/gauge. Boats and boat trailers can be moved (although size is an issue and must be resolved advance); they do count against your weight allowance. All issues must be worked out with the shipper on a case-by-case basis.

Claims for Damage

Despite the best efforts of your carrier in moving your goods and your own vigilance in providing quality assurance, your belongings may suffer some damage during a move. If they do, you have every right to file a claim, with a maximum payment of $40,000 for the entire shipment. Additionally, there are limits on individual items, ranging from $50 for candles to $20,000 for an automobile (shipped for overseas moves only), and a few items are not "claimable" at all, including bank or stock certificates, war trophies, anything you damage yourself, private business items, or property illegally acquired. These limits change frequently, so check with your PPSO before each move. If you are moving more than $40,000 worth of personal property, you may want to obtain supplementary personal property insurance from a private insurer. USAA has a good package, as do several other insurance companies. It can be purchased for year-round protection or limited to transits and moves. You can also increase maximum protection limits or arrange for full replacement (not the normally depreciated value) with the government by paying an extra charge. Discuss it with your counselor when setting up the move, because you must decide at that point—once the move is booked with the carrier, the additional governmentally purchased insurance will not be available. Also, such insurance is not available from the government on moves overseas or to Hawaii.

Filing a claim is not very complicated. First, bear in mind that both the government and the carrier have the right to inspect anything that is broken, so don't simply throw these items away when you discover them. Make a pile of "broken stuff" in the garage, and tag any scuff marks, scratches, or damage to larger pieces. You must clearly note on the arrival inventory any breakage or damage and sign the form provided by the carrier, which is called a DD Form 1840, "Joint Statement of Loss or Damage at Delivery." If you do not list missing or damaged items, you may lose the chance to recover, so take your time. Naturally, you may discover damage after everything is unpacked and the movers have gone, so ask for a copy of DD Form 1840R, "Notice of Loss or Damage." You must notify the PPSO via submission of the appropriate form within seventy days. Remember, *notation of loss or damage on the carrier's inventory or any other form is not acceptable for processing a claim; you must file DD Forms 1840/1840R.*

After you file your initial Form 1840/1840R with the government, you will receive a package of paperwork to fill out to place your claim. You will have two years from the date of damage to submit the claim, but the sooner the better. You will have to certify the age of your damaged property, the value, and in some cases provide estimates of value or cost of repairs. The forms are largely self-explanatory, but the counselors at your PPSO can guide you through any problem areas. Although it is troublesome and somewhat time consuming to file the forms, make the effort—if your property has suffered damage, you deserve the financial reimbursement, and the process helps keep carriers honest and ensures that they do their best. The government will generally contact the carrier and recover most (if not all) of what is paid out to you, so the entire process of sending forward a claim forms a circle of responsibility and helps assure that good carriers succeed and that the less effective lose the government's business.

Remember that you must exhaust any commercial coverage you have prior to applying to the government for reimbursement. You cannot under any circumstances collect twice for the same damage.

Pets

Naturally, you will want to move your pets. The bad news, of course, is that the DoD is not obligated to provide any assistance in moving your basset hound, "Emma," or whoever your pet may be. Record the expenses you incur (which may be considerable) when moving your pet because they are tax deductible, although you will receive no direct compensation for them.

You also need to be familiar with the pet-related laws of the new state to which you are moving. There may be requirements for up-to-date shots (rabies, for example), as well as health certificates for more exotic "pets" (e.g., horses). Your base veterinarian should be able to provide advice before you begin the journey.

When moving overseas or to Hawaii, moving your pet can become very complicated. Some locations (United Kingdom, Hawaii) have long quarantine requirements (up to six months) to ensure rabies does not enter the country or state. Although this is being reduced to thirty days in most cases, your veterinarian can provide additional information. You may be able to arrange transportation for Emma on government air within the continental United States for a nominal fee or simply transport her by car; more likely you will need to make all arrangements and pay all expenses on your own.

Cars and Mobile Homes

Within the United States, the government will pay you to drive one (or two) cars, depending on your circumstances. Your PSA or disbursing office can explain the rules, which revolve around the timing of your sailor's arrival and the rest of the family, as well as the total number of people involved. The government will also allow you to drive a mobile home as an alternative to the standard family car (or POV, privately owned vehicle). If you have a mobile home that cannot be driven, you can make special arrangements with the PPSO. This can become very complicated, with alternatives for moving the mobile home with furniture in it or empty, by the government or privately. Explore these options carefully with your carrier if you own a mobile home.

Do-It-Yourself Moves

If you are a young and carefree navy spouse without a lot of personal property, you and your sailor may want to do the packing and moving yourself—and you can make a nice profit for the work. This is called a "Do-It-Yourself Move," or DITY (pronounced "ditty") move. You apply to execute a DITY move at the PPSO. The counselor will estimate the cost to the government of moving you, then award you 80 percent of that amount. If you can move the goods for less, you pocket the difference. If the move costs more than 80 percent of the commercial price, but less than the entire cost, the government will make sure you break even. Only if the move costs more than the government's 100 percent estimate will you be stuck with the difference.

DITY moves can be a very good deal, and many people earn several hundred dollars executing this. After your counselor has determined how much the government would pay, estimate the cost of packing, renting a moving van, and moving yourself. You may find yourself pleasantly surprised. Obviously, if you have large pieces of furniture or a lot of personal property, it would be too difficult, but it is a great option when you are just starting out.

Some things to consider when contemplating a DITY move:

• Decide what method of transportation to use for your shipments (your own car or a rental). You cannot use UPS or Federal Express.

• Paperwork must be done in advance. Contact the PPSO before you go too far in the planning process.

• You will need weight tickets for all vehicles used in the DITY move, including ID, weight scale used, and so forth. The PPSO can help suggest a place for the weighing.

• Consider insurance coverage. Since a DITY move is not considered within the scope of your sailor's employment, you could be held liable in an accident.

• After the move, you have to file any damage claims within forty-five days. Keep a copy of all submitted claims.

Travel Pay, Allowances, and Benefits

There are a wide variety of special payments, allowances, and benefits associated with moving. Specifics can be obtained by your sailor through the command's disbursing office or the base PSD, but the following are a few to keep in mind.

Transportation Expenses

The military will reimburse you for the mileage between duty stations at a set rate per mile if you are driving your personal vehicles. The exact amount varies per the number of people involved in the move: seventeen cents per mile for just you and your spouse, nineteen cents for the two of you and one dependent, and twenty cents for more than that. Driving is generally the most economical way to travel. The government will pay for two cars, and you can petition for a third under special circumstances.

As an alternative, the government will reimburse the cost of direct, timely, and appropriate airplane, train, or hired conveyance (bus) travel. If you are considering this option, check with disbursing before buying any commercial tickets of any kind to ensure they are reimbursable.

During the period of the travel, the government will generally authorize the payment of a per diem allowance for food and lodging on the road, whether you drive yourself, fly, or ride a train.

Dislocation

Because government payments for moves and travel generally do not cover permanent change of station (PCS) costs, there is a dislocation allowance paid, which amounts to two months of basic allowance for quarters. Your disbursing office can provide details on obtaining it. While not universally available (for example, first duty station moves do not apply), this is a great deal.

Temporary Lodging

When moving to or from overseas, an allowance called temporary lodging allowance is paid, which will vary depending on the area's cost of living. Here in the United States a similar payment, temporary lodging expense, can be collected for up to ten days (a maximum of $110 per day) for housing coverage at the beginning or end of a stateside move.

House Hunting

The government will authorize up to ten days for house hunting, although there will be no financial support for the house-hunting trip. Be sure to take advantage of this.

Proceed Time

Proceed time is the time the government allocates to you during a PCS move, and it is in addition to days authorized for the travel between PCS stations. The government generally will provide one to four days of proceed time. Your PPSO will have the details.

Leave between Duty Stations

Your sailor's orders generally will specify an amount of "delay in reporting," sometimes referred to as DelRep. This is simply the amount of time he or she is allowed to take leave. Your sailor will have to work this out with both the departing and gaining commands, and it can vary from thirty days (but don't count on it) to zero—it depends on your sailor's skills and who is being relieved at the next station.

Useful Publications, Telephone Numbers, and Web Sites

Lodging

An excellent publication to help you with your move is *Guide to Military Installations,* which is revised each spring as a free supplement to *Navy Times.* It includes information on places to stay worldwide and can normally be found at Family Service Centers or base libraries. If you have difficulty finding the *Navy Times* supplement or you require a little more detail, *Guide to Military Installations Worldwide* by Military Times Newsweekly Group, publishers of *Navy Times,* is available in book form and is updated about every two years.

You can always stay at Navy Inns (also known as Navy Lodges) on a priority basis if you are on PCS orders. Make your reservations as early as possible and be prepared to show a copy of your orders when you check in. You can make, confirm, change, or cancel a reservation on the Navy Exchange web site <http://www.navy-nex.com/lodge/index.html>. Or, if you do not have access to a computer, telephone numbers for reservations follow: navy at 1-800-628-9466, air force at 1-888-235-6343, and army 1-800-462-7691.

Shipping Vehicles

A good web site for all the service options is <http://www.mtmc.army.mil>, which is coordinated by the Military Traffic Management Command. This web site also lists telephone numbers for all vehicle shipping centers. Currently, you can only ship a vehicle overseas, although there is discussion of expanding this benefit to domestic shipping of a single car.

Installations

The Defense Manpower Data Center, operated by the Department of Defense, operates a web site at <http://www.dmdc.osd.mil>. This is also a great way to find out general information about a base where you might be moving. Click on "sites" and be prepared to provide limited personal information such as your name, birth date, and social security number. The system will then match this information against the DEERS data base (see chapter 2) to ensure that only authorized personnel are accessing the information.

Allowances, Benefits, and Moving Issues

The Department of Defense's Defense Technical Information Center <http://www.dtic.mil> includes detailed information on allowances, benefits, and moving issues. Click on "Find It," scroll down and click on "Per Diem, Travel and Transportation Allowance Committee," and "Other Sites."

You can also find a lot of great moving information and other navy-specific issues on the LIFELines web site <http://www.lifelines2000.org>, as discussed in chapter 3.

Conclusion

Moving is perhaps the most difficult thing for navy spouses, but it is also the most exciting. If you like moving, in the end you will probably like the navy. Try to stay positive, ask for advice from friends in the area with more experience, stay in touch with your sponsor at the new command, and, as always, look for the humor in life. You *will* find that new veterinarian, your sixth grader will make the select soccer team, and Emma will love her new yard. And so will you.

A Checklist for Moving upon Receiving Orders

• Visit your NFSC and gather any helpful material about your new duty station.

• Contact the PPSO for an appointment to ship your household goods. Set this up as early as possible—no later than three months before your desired move date, especially if you will be moving in the summer high-demand period.

• Write or call your sponsor at the new command. If your sponsor has not replied within thirty days after orders are written, have your sailor get in touch with the command master chief at the new command.

• Notify your landlord or housing office of the departure date.

• Investigate key information in the new area: schools, housing, medical care, EFM.

About Three Months before the Move

• Take a house-hunting trip to your new command. You don't need to use leave to do this, because the navy will authorize up to ten days of permissive temporary duty for house hunting.

• Start keeping careful track of all expenses for income tax purposes.

• Inventory everything you own, preferably both in writing and with a video camera. Keep this with you in case of total, catastrophic loss of your goods in the move. Identify those items (jewelry, computers, family albums) that you do not want the movers to move and think about how you will move them.

• Make any final medical, dental, or optical appointments in your current area.

• Draw up a power of attorney if the move will cause a separation requiring one.

• Make reservations for temporary lodging (the Navy Lodge) at the new location.

About Two Months before the Move

• Make any vacation arrangements that are involved with the move to the new location. Use navy lodges and other military temporary lodging while traveling between duty stations. The "Guide to U.S. Military Installations," an annual supplement to the *Navy Times,* is very helpful. It should be available at the exchange or in the base library.

• Have your vehicles tuned and inspected.

• Check your insurance coverage.

• Make pet arrangements. If moving overseas, make sure you have all local regulations and a plan for quarantine if required.

About a Month before the Move

• Notify schools of your move and arrange to pick up records and ask for procedures for sending them on as required.

• Check ID card and DEER enrollment.

• Make a list of key telephone numbers.

• Check the arrangements your PPSO has made for your move. Give them a call.

• Have an extensive garage sale and giveaway to charity. Try to get rid of anything you really don't need, or you will find yourself very discouraged at the new duty station unwrapping the unwanted items.

• Pack away items that require special packing.

• Confirm reservations along the route and at the new location.

About Three Weeks before the Move

• Finalize pet travel arrangements.

• Back up computer files on disk.

• Begin separating and prepacking items at home. Note professional books and other items that don't count against your weight allowance if weight is a factor for you.

• Decide on your "cleaning and exit strategy." If you are in government quarters, the best approach usually is to hire a cleaning service to come in and clean the quarters. Ask around the neighborhood or the housing office for a reputable service with a good track record of passing inspections. The cost will be around one hundred dollars or so, depending on the size of your quarters. If you are a renter in the local civilian economy, you may want to consider doing the work yourself to save money. Again, this depends on the standards of your landlord, the cost of the cleaning service, your own time availability, and a host of other factors. In general, if you can afford it, the money is wisely spent having a cleaning service come in, since you will be very busy during the last few days.

About Two Weeks before the Move

• Dispose of flammable liquids such as spray paints, solvents, thinners, gas, and oil.

• Set up the final cleaning and walk-through of your house.

• Close out your safety deposit box, if you have one.

• Set aside cleaning materials to be used after packing and loading.

• Reconfirm your cleaning date with the cleaning service, if you hire one.

• Pick up any personal items that are with merchants—dry cleaning, photos.

• Arrange for disconnection of all utilities, stop newspaper and mail delivery, and have your mail forwarded. The post office has forwarding kits.

• Make sure you have worked out a means to pay final bills and to have existing bills reach you while you are in transit. One way is to forward mail to the new command; another is to send it to parents or friends.

About One Week before the Move

• Pick up medical and dental records to hand carry.

• Work out child care for moving day—you don't want little ones around underfoot.

• Clean the "big ticket" items at your house—freezer, refrigerator, stove. Don't use them after they have been cleaned.

• Call the movers to confirm their day and time of arrival. If there is any confusion, work it out with the transportation office where you set up your move.

• Confirm cleaning service appointment one last time.

Moving Day

• Get up early, get ready for the movers. A nice touch is to offer them coffee and doughnuts, but don't feel obligated. You might also offer to make a run for fast food for lunch or have pizza delivered. They will appreciate it. Never offer beer or alcohol. Have sodas available. Little things count.

• Watch the movers closely. This is your furniture, after all. Verify the inventory carefully.

• Double-check that the things you don't want moved are cordoned off in some secure part of the house, or locked in your car (papers, jewelry, computers, cash, etc.).

• Don't let the movers simply mark "scratched" on the inventory. Have them specify the location of the scratch. They may add other scratches, and an inventory signed by you will allow them to get away with it.

• Call the PPSO at least once with a progress report. Ask if they intend to send an inspector over for a quality assurance visit. Let them know you are involved and have their number. Also know their after-hours duty number in case the move runs long.

• Leave your home only after the moving truck has departed.

After the Move

• Execute your "cleaning and exit strategy," either by doing the cleaning yourself or by having the cleaning service come in.

• Clear with your landlord or the base inspector for quarters.

• Depart the area.

Table 6.1. Weight Allowances

Rank	Limit, in pounds, for shipping or storing personal goods for PCS moves	
	Without dependents	With dependents
O-6 to O-10	18,000	18,000
O-5, W-5	16,000	17,500
O-4, W-4	14,000	17,000
O-3, W-3	13,000	14,500
O-2, W-2	12,500	13,500
O-1, W-1	10,000	12,000
E-9	12,000	14,500
E-8	11,000	13,500
E-7	10,500	12,500
E-6	8,000	11,000
E-5	7,000	9,000
E-4 over 2 yr svc	7,000	8,000
E-4 under 2 yr svc	3,500	7,000
E-3[a]	2,000	5,000
E-2[a]	1,500	5,000
E-1[a]	1,500	5,000

Source: U.S. Navy
[a] E-3, E-2, and E-1 married to an E-3, E-2, or E-1 can receive a total weight allowance of 5,000 pounds, if both have zero dependents.

7
An Ocean Away

I cannot rest from travel; I will drink
Life to the lees. All times I have enjoyed.

. . . .

Yet all experience is an arch where through
Gleams that untraveled world whose margin fades
Forever and forever when I move.

"Ulysses"
Alfred Lord Tennyson

Overseas Duty

All right, I admit it—I love living overseas.

As a navy junior, I lived twice in overseas locations, both times in Europe. For the first tour I was very young; for the second, I was in a DoD high school. Both were wonderful experiences for my family and certainly were career highlights for my father. As for me, I had a chance to travel all over Europe by the time I was seventeen. Throughout my years as a navy spouse, my husband and I have looked at overseas duty as an option, but the assignment has not come our way—yet. The vast majority of our friends who have lived overseas have enjoyed the experience and freely shared their collective wisdom for this chapter.

The Bureau of Naval Personnel will tell career navy people that they can expect one overseas tour in a twenty-year career, with overseas being defined here as "outside of the continental United States" (i.e., including Hawaii and Alaska), referred to as CONUS (pronounced "cone-us"). The most "typical" overseas assignments for navy people are Hawaii, Japan, and Europe. Additionally, there are many navy members in smaller locations around the world, from Guam to Singapore to Alaska to Central America.

Living overseas is challenging, but the rewards are exceptional. In a sense, both the good aspects and the challenges of navy life are magnified across the board. You and your children will be exposed to a completely new culture, language, customs, transportation system, communications—all of this will be interesting, broadening, and occasionally maddening. Schools will always be available to your children, usually through the DoD, taught in English at the same standards (or better) than in CONUS. Shopping will vary widely from fully stocked exchanges and commissaries to small local markets. I will discuss this in more detail below, but the point is simple: you can spend your time fruitlessly complaining, because "it isn't the same as back in Norfolk" or you can seize the day and say, "This is exciting and different—I love it."

I recommend the latter approach, and in this chapter I will show how taking such an approach can work for you and your family with fewer problems and pitfalls.

Bienvenue (welcome) to overseas duty.

Overseas Screening

Moving overseas will begin much like all other navy moves, with your sailor coming home one night, a little distracted, and starting the dinner conversation with, "Well, I got through to the detailer today, and it looks like we'll be moving to . . . Japan."

Panic.

Once you have recovered from the initial shock of going overseas, and after you have found Sasebo on a map of Japan in your seventeen-year-old atlas, the next step is *not* to buy a samurai sword, a geisha outfit, or tickets on Nippon Airlines. Instead, you will be involved in something called overseas screening.

While this is a slightly inconvenient and seemingly intrusive procedure, it is designed to ensure that our navy sends overseas only the kinds of families who are squared away and organized, healthy and financially secure; this in turn ensures that there are fewer problems for those who go. Your sailor's personnel office will manage the process of overseas screening, but you and your sailor will be very involved as well—from providing financial disclosures to obtaining physicals for everyone in the family. The checks involved in overseas screening include finding out whether you have:

- an EFM, that is, a child or other family member who is handicapped, has a special medical condition, or has a particular set of needs that would be hard to fulfill overseas
- family advocacy needs or issues
- substance abuse problems
- financial stability and responsibility
- psychiatric disorders
- medical and/or dental conditions
- pregnancy that could affect travel and assignment

Your sailor will also receive a special screening to ensure there are no problems for him or her with regard to obesity, physical readiness (i.e., did your sailor pass the physical readiness test), disciplinary records, and HIV screening. The process will conclude with a signature by the CO certifying that the process has been completed and that your sailor and the entire family are ready to go overseas.

Overseas screening is a detailed process, done for *your* protection. Work honestly, openly, and promptly with the people at the personnel office. Screening should be started *immediately* upon receipt of orders. The process will also take you through the more mundane aspects of moving overseas, including immunizations, passport requirements, dental checkups, and so forth.

Resources and Information

One of the best sources of information about moving overseas will be your command sponsor at the new duty station. As soon as your sailor receives orders, the overseas duty station (who will have received notification at the same time) will assign a "command sponsor." While this is true for any move, it is particularly important for an overseas move. Your new sponsor should contact your sailor very quickly, and offer the following:

- a welcome-aboard package with plenty of important information about moving overseas

- telephone numbers at work and home

- points of contact at the new location (housing, medical, dental) for advance liaison

- advice on key aspects of the move: whether to bring a car, the availability of housing, the school situation for your children, types of things you will want to stock up on before moving (electrical adapters for your appliances, for example), and so forth

If you have not heard from a new command sponsor within thirty days of receipt of orders, ask your sailor to contact the personnel office at the new command and get the process "jump-started." A command sponsor is the single most important source of information you will have. If the sponsor is married (and he or she should be, since your sailor is), get the number of the spouse and call right away. Go to the NFSC and use their telephone, because the call can be expensive—but call and check in with them for information and guidance early.

Meanwhile, you should be trying to find another reliable navy spouse in your present region who has recent experience in the overseas duty assignment to which you are headed. You can call your command om-budsman for this information. Also check with the NFSC—they will know of families who are arriving in your area fresh off a tour from overseas. Likewise, ask your navy friends, and have your sailor do the same—I guarantee that within twenty inquiries you will find someone who has lived in that location fairly recently. This is particularly true for large overseas destinations—Hawaii, Japan, and Italy. Some of the questions to ask include the key aspects of an overseas move mentioned above, as well as advice on specific locations for living, how to get a telephone in-stalled, what the schools are like, how they liked it, the hardest part about living there—essentially the same questions you would have about mov-ing anywhere. Ask also for any old maps, pamphlets, or other printed in-formation. A note of caution here: some people don't like living overseas, so if you run into a fellow navy spouse who is negative about where you are headed, don't let it throw you—you will certainly find many others who enjoyed it. Take advice from many different sources, be prepared, and recognize that in the end you will have to form your own conclu-sions and judgments after you have lived in your new location awhile.

Additionally, you should hit the local or base library for information about your new location. The base library might have a separate file of good information about the location from the perspective of service people who have lived there. You should also invest in a recent guidebook about the location. Any bookstore will carry this, but you may want to check what is available in the library first to see which books appeal to you most—I like the Fodor's series, but there are several other good ones as well.

The navy and associated support organizations publish several useful booklets, notably *Overseasmanship* by the Naval Services Family-Line. These provide information to help you prepare for overseas assignments. You can find a copy at the NFSC, you can call the associa-tion directly at 202-433-2333, or you can access their web site at <http://www.lifelines2000.org/familyline/home.asp>. You will also find other excellent printed resources there. In addition, both the *All Hands* and *Navy Times* have plenty of information about living overseas. Try the base library for back copies.

Still another excellent resource is the Overseas Transfer Information Service, at 1-800-327-8197 (or call collect at 703-697-6621/34). Manned by the Bureau of Naval Personnel, it answers your questions and pro-vides advice during working hours.

The Overseas Moving Process

Once you know you are going overseas, the next step, as usual, is to set up your move. There are special aspects to moving overseas that will be discussed in detail with you at the PPSO. They vary widely depending on location, but some things to be aware of are as follows.

Moving Your Belongings

Your goods will be taken by truck to a port in the United States, then by ship overseas. This can take time. Be prepared to live for a period of time without your goods. This will not be as hard as you may think, since your new command is accustomed to such situations and will have solutions available (check with your command sponsor).

Shipping Your Car

This will be a new experience. Like your other belongings, your car will be shipped overseas after you take it to a designated port. In some instances it may make better sense not to ship a car at all—you may be better off using public transportation or buying a used car when you arrive. If you do decide to take one, the government will pay for its shipping. You will need to check with your insurance company about coverage, both for the shipping process and for driving in the new country. Also check on the availability of unleaded gas at your destination—the PPSO and your sponsor there should be able to answer most of your questions. Also, the excellent government publication, *It's Your Move*, available at any PPSO, has detailed information on many important topics involving military moves.

Taking Your Pets

Pets can be a challenge. Some overseas locations will not permit you to bring animals in at all, for fear of bringing in rabies and other animal diseases. Other destinations will require a lengthy stay in a kennel to ensure they don't have rabies or any other communicable disease. For example, Hawaii requires a six-month quarantine. Your base veterinarian can give you all information on pet requirements. Additionally, the government will not pay for shipping your pet, and very few Air Mobility Command (AMC) flights are available for pets. Does this mean you have to give away or board your basset hound, Emma? Of course not. It simply means you should be prepared for some extra research and cost to get her to your new home overseas. For instance, AMC, if available, will ship up to two dogs and cats in cargo; they also require a small fee and have a one-hundred-pound-weight limit. Alternatively, you can use a commercial airliner, although each airline has its own rules. You always will need medical certifications, particularly a rabies vaccination.

Moving your family pet overseas can be a challenge. Author's collection.

Housing Overseas

Housing arrangements vary widely from country to country overseas, but really the choices are not that different from those in the United States. In general, you will have to wait to get into quarters, and the sooner you are put on the housing list the better. There will be off-base housing opportunities that may be very expensive or quite reasonable, depending on the country; the houses can vary from tiny, hyperexpensive row houses in Japan to beautiful villas in Italy or Bahrain. Your command sponsor is the best source of information in this regard. You have several options while waiting for quarters, ranging from staying at a local hotel or lodging place for several months, to bringing the family only after you have found a place. Again, the receiving command will be experienced in handling this and will provide detailed guidance to you through the command sponsor.

Because there are differences in overseas costs of living, and problems with expensive housing, the government has two programs designed to help you as you move overseas. The first is called the overseas housing allowance (OHA), which is for people living off base. It is paid in addition to BAH, and is paid worldwide. Payment will cover the entire rent as well as utilities. It is the overseas equivalent of the old stateside VHA, and is obviously keyed to the specific area in which you live. You will fill out the appropriate forms at your new command.

A second stipend is the cost of living allowance, which is a payment made to bring your salary in line with local living conditions. COLA, as it is commonly called, varies with the number of people in the family, the location, and the rank of your sailor. It is adjusted as currency fluctuates, and also reduced if you and your family are receiving meals from the government. COLA can add up to a considerable sum of money, but you need to adjust your budget accordingly so you don't spend it all on luxury items when the money (more than $3,000 in some places) rolls in each month. Remember, that money will roll out just a quickly as you pay for basic goods and services in expensive countries such as Japan.

Schools

Relax—the DoD operates an extensive network of overseas schools to ensure that your children receive an education comparable to (in fact, largely better than) what they would receive stateside. The schools run from K–12, with some preschool instruction available in selected locations. My own experiences in DoD schools have been terrific, and most of our friends have found the same. Your child will be in a safe and homogeneous environment with wonderful resources for learning a foreign language, culture, history, and geography at their fingertips.

There are over 70,000 students in nearly 160 DoD schools around the world, although they are clustered in only thirteen countries. Attendance at the schools is free for any children who are "command sponsored," meaning they are in the country as part of official travel orders. If the children are not command sponsored—that is, your sailor is on "unaccompanied" orders but you and the children went anyway; they can attend on a space-available basis. There is no cost for this option as well. Every school in the DoD system is fully accredited through the North Central Association of Colleges and Schools. There are advance-placement courses available in many of the schools, and there is a highly regarded boarding school in England available if your sailor is in a remote location. If you are not interested in the boarding school option, you can petition for reimbursement to send your children to local private schools, which are nearly always available in English for the diplomatic community.

Although the likelihood of being sent overseas with special-needs children is remote, it is possible that you may discover one of your children has learning or physical problems while overseas. The overseas DoD schools provide service for children in this situation.

Before your overseas move, obtain more information on schooling by writing the director of the Department of Defense Education Activity, 4040 N. Fairfax Drive, Arlington, Virginia, 22203-2635. Or you can call the main telephone number, 703-696-4235. For special-needs situations, the number is 703-696-4492.

Language

If you are stationed in another country, make an effort to learn the language. One of the best experiences of living overseas will be your interaction—haltingly at first, of course—with the inhabitants of another culture and country. Remember, as a guest in their country, the most gracious thing you can do is learn at least some basics such as "please," "thank you," "how are you," and so forth.

There are many ways to do this. First, for some assignments, your sailor will receive language training. If so, see if you can attend or receive some training yourself. Second, the navy offers language tapes (worth hundreds of dollars) for people moving overseas. Have your sailor check with the base education office. Third, base and local libraries will have sets of tapes and books to help you learn the local language. And if you have a home computer, there are programs for most modern languages available as well. Finally, don't forget to include your children. Nothing will make your first few months in a new country easier than knowing at least a little of the language. Bear in mind, too, that English is increasingly becoming a universal language, so there probably will be at least a few English speakers just about everywhere. So don't be intimidated.

As you learn a new language, you may want to reciprocate. In some countries (Japan, parts of Europe), the locals are willing to hire navy

Living overseas can keep you slightly off balance, but in the end you will enjoy yourself. Author's collection.

spouses to teach English. This generally consists of going to a classroom and speaking to small groups of people so they can practice their English and perfect their accents. Your base NFSC or new command ombudsman will have information on this simple and easy way to interact with the people of your new country, and to make a little money as well.

Enjoying Yourself after Arrival

Moving to another country—and facing the unknown—can be a daunting prospect. But once you get there, meet with your command sponsor, and begin the process of settling in, you should get a chance to catch your breath and enjoy yourself, even as you await the arrival of household goods and your automobile.

This is a great time to get out and explore your new surroundings. Go with the spouse of the command sponsor, or check with the command ombudsman of your sailor's new assignment. Start by finding your way to appropriate medical and dental service areas, both routine and emergency. Then a trip to the children's school is in order, to register if you have moved in the summer, or to get the children started if you have been forced to move during the school year (which is unlikely, as the vast majority of overseas moves are made during the summer). Find out where the best U.S.-style shopping (exchange and commissary) are located. Learn where most of the Americans live and where they socialize. Try to adjust your sailor's schedule so that he or she arrives with at least ten days of leave before checking in and your sailor can be part of this process. Doing all of this will ensure that you have covered the "little America" aspects of living in your new environment, and it should not take more than a few days—a week at the most.

Now the fun begins. Start taking morning or afternoon forays out into the new country around you. Go at first with the "old hands" who are experienced in the new location—go for shopping, lunch, a dinner excursion with the entire family. Find the best of the local markets and experience the sights and sounds and smells of the new country. Learn where locals go for coffee, tea, or cocktails; try new foods, from Japanese sushi (bits of raw fish and vegetables on rice), to German schnitzel, to the seafood pizzas of Naples' wood-burning brick ovens. Expand and practice your language skills, and almost everywhere you go, you will be heartened by the friendly reception you receive.

After a few weeks of getting your feet on the ground with day trips, you will be ready to sit down with your sailor and the children and plan an overnight visit to somewhere off the beaten path. Go for a weekend at the beach south of Sydney, or take the train to Tokyo. Grab a hydrofoil across the Bay of Naples to the Amalfi coast, or go on a weekend ski trip to the German Alps. You can get ideas and information from the recreational services people at the local base, or by talking with those who have been around awhile. Eventually, you will want to vacation in your region, taking the entire family for a week-long trip somewhere— perhaps to Singapore from Japan, or to France from Germany. Check with those who are already in place for information on the availability of MAC flights (see the section on "Military Flights" below) to cut your costs. Expand your area of knowledge and experience—this is a superb opportunity to learn much more about the world around you. At the same time, you will be performing a valuable service to the United States by being a goodwill ambassador abroad, showing others what our country is all about.

Military Flights

While living overseas, you probably will be very interested in securing military flights to go home on occasion. If there is extra space available on a military flight, you can often "take a hop" with the military. While the rules vary a little from base to base, the fundamentals are the same. The military offers "space-A" (space available) flights for active-duty and retired military personnel and their dependents to and from the United States on a regular basis.

First, there is no reservation system. The flights are never guaranteed, and the seats are apportioned on a priority system, with a first-come, first-served basis. The basic priorities include the following categories:

Category 1: service members, family members, and DoD civilians on emergency leave

Category 2: service members on environmental and morale leave and family members accompanying them

Category 3: service members and family members on regular leave; also for service members who are on permissive temporary duty for house hunting

Category 4: military families on environmental and morale leave (without the service member)

Category 5: service members on permissive temporary duty (other than house hunting); general travel by family members

Category 6: retired military members and their families; reserves; ROTC students

A pamphlet detailing these categories is available at most Air Mobility Command terminals.

To sign up for a AMC flight, you will need to present yourself in person initially, leaving a telephone number where you can be reached. You will then be called when your flight is preparing for departure. Some passenger terminals will accept a request by fax. The numbers for all worldwide passenger terminals are available in several different publications, including the annual *Navy Times* supplement on worldwide installations. A list is also available at the base library or the NFSC. You can sign up for five destinations at once. Be prepared to pay for your food and lodging in an area while waiting for your flight to be called, and never depend on a space-A flight if you absolutely must be somewhere at a certain time—missions change, flights are frequently canceled or rescheduled, and it is always possible you will be bumped by someone with a higher priority. The AMC web site is <http://www.public.scot.af. mil/hqamc>.

Conclusion

Being an American abroad means being sensitive to the perceptions that other countries have about the United States. The term "ugly American" has been used to describe U.S. citizens who travel and live abroad and leave an unpleasant impression on others. The stereotype of the American is that of a rude, big-spending, arrogant, and egotistical individual. Keep in mind that citizens of other countries are not always comfortable with the image of the United States as a superpower with global reach. You can help counteract any bad impressions with your day-to-day courtesy, interest and respect for other cultures, and enthusiasm for living abroad.

The excitement of living overseas is what the navy means when it says, "The Navy: It's Not Just a Job, It's an Adventure." Life can be an adventure—if you let it. But if you restrict yourself to the "little America" side of life while abroad—as many people sadly and inexplicably do— you will give up the very best part of being overseas in the service. So go forth, be a good ambassador for your country, and—above all—enjoy this experience of a lifetime.

8
Ideals, Beliefs, and Personal Challenges

Two Roads diverged in a wood, and I—
I took the one less traveled by,
And that has made all the difference.
"The Road Not Taken"
Robert Frost

Rules of the Road

In order to ensure that ships can maneuver safely at sea, the maritime community has developed a code of conduct for the safe operations of ships entitled "The Rules of the Road." It is a very detailed and specific codification of how ships should turn, operate, sound signals, and—in general—behave around other ships.

Perhaps unfortunately, there is not a detailed "Rules of the Road" for being a navy spouse. But there *is* the accumulated knowledge of thousands of navy spouses who have preceded you through the very interesting life in which you are engaged today. In this chapter I will discuss some of the nonspecific but important information that will help you be an effective—and happy—navy spouse while leading a demanding life.

This is not to say there is a set of "rules" that cannot be broken. Far from it. There is a tremendous (and very healthy) diversity among the many different navy spouses involved in our service today. But a basic understanding of what navy people generally think and expect can be helpful to a navy spouse.

Courage, Honor, Commitment

Certainly a good place to start our discussion is with the navy's stated "core values" of courage, honor, and commitment. These simple principles are the distillation of over two hundred years of American navy tradition, and they are continually emphasized throughout the navy world.

What do they mean?

Courage is something a navy spouse needs in great measure. Think of the frequent separations from your sailor, which require a great deal of courage and true grit to deal with. Next, there are the constant moves, often around the world, frequently made on short notice. It takes courage to move into a new neighborhood every couple of years. And most important, there is the need for courage when your sailor is sailing into harm's way in the service of the country. The last scenario will not happen often, but when it does, it calls for resources of courage you may have to dig deep to find. But you will.

Honor is a simple word, but it carries an enormous burden of meaning. All members of the navy, and I would include spouses in that number, should do all they can to conduct themselves in the highest ethical manner at all times. Try always to be honest and truthful; a good starting point is the honor code of the U.S. Naval Academy, which states that a person should not "lie, cheat, or steal." At the end of the day, honor is the most important thing any of us owns, and it is the foundation for the way the world views us.

Commitment, quite simply, is at the heart of your life as a navy spouse. It takes commitment to stay the course and support your sailor in the challenges of a navy career. You are part of a team, from the most junior seaman to the most senior admiral—and including all spouses, friends, and family members—that must work together to make America's navy successful. And whether you are part of it for just the few years of your sailor's "hitch" or for the decades-long career of a senior admiral, you will need commitment to make your association with the navy an enjoyable and meaningful experience.

Attitude

So much of life is in the way you lead it. In some ways, the world is like a mirror—it will reflect back at you what you put into it. If you are whining, short-tempered, and negative, you may be amazed at how many unpleasant people seem to surround you. On the other hand, if you smile, make life an adventure, and keep your sense of humor, you will meet like-minded people taking the same approach.

The key is to distinguish between something that is truly *wrong* and should be addressed, challenged, and corrected, and something that is unpleasant (such as a deployment) but which is in fact an understood, accepted, and normal part of the navy experience.

Dealing with Deployments

The most common irritant you will face in navy life is forward deployment. It is without question the worst part of navy life from a spouse's

A navy couple is saddened by the prospect of an imminent deployment. U.S. Naval Institute collection.

viewpoint. You will be without the love, support, and daily presence of the most important person in your life. There will be times when you are lonely, afraid, and saddened by that void. But here are some ideas for coping with deployment by developing a better attitude about it.

First, you must accept it. The deployment is part of navy life, your spouse's chosen profession. Complaining about it will accomplish nothing and will put your spouse in a difficult situation.

Second, try to look at a deployment as an opportunity. "For what?" you may ask. For the personal growth that comes with being forced to take over completely the running of the household. Meeting and overcoming challenges is one of the most rewarding aspects of life. There is also the opportunity to travel. Many navy spouses take advantage of a deployment to fly over and visit their sailors, and I encourage all navy spouses to pursue this. If you have small children, line up baby-sitting (grandparents are perfect), take vacation time from your job, and jump on an airplane to join your spouse overseas. Most ships are very accommodating, making a deployment a terrific chance to enjoy a second honeymoon in romantic settings.

Third, you must work hard to maintain what might be called "connectivity" with your spouse. There are several key ways to do this, which we will discuss in the next section.

Deployment Connectivity

Connectivity is the sum of communications and commitment. Both must be emphasized throughout a long deployment, and there are a number of important ways to undertake each.

Communications can be through a wide variety of mediums, such as the telephone, class easy messages and telegrams (Western Union), USOGrams, e-mail, and letters (all covered in chapter 4). Here, we will focus on how to use each means (rather than the mechanics of them) in maintaining connectivity.

Telephone calls are the best means of communication, obviously. Hearing your spouse's voice is always a treat, and although calls can be very expensive, it is often worth the money. A few tips to bear in mind about telephone calls on cruise: First, try to remain upbeat and positive on the line. Your spouse will not want to hear about your daily trials and tribulations; instead, mention how much you miss your sailor and cannot wait for him or her to return, and talk about the fun things you will do when that happens. Don't use the telephone for problem solving if you can avoid it. There will be times when that is necessary, but try to reserve telephone time for love, reassurance, and talking about being together again.

Second, suggest that your sailor make it a point to call each time the unit reaches port during a long deployment. This will help make the passage of time on the cruise easier, and it gives you a window to the interesting foreign ports they are visiting. If your sailor can call from sea, try to set up a time for the call in advance, perhaps with a USOGram, and keep that time free. Don't be distraught if your sailor misses the opportunity—there may be an operational window that has interfered. Just try to set up a regular call every couple of weeks from sea if that is feasible.

Third, watch the costs and adjust accordingly. Make sure your spouse carries a calling card before leaving and that he or she uses it—not the hotel or bar telephone—to call you. Your sailor should try to use a toll-free, automated calling service rather than an operator. Make sure your spouse checks with someone senior on the ship who has been around—perhaps a chief or limited duty officer (LDO)—about how to make the least expensive telephone calls. A five hundred dollar telephone bill is not something you want to receive during a deployment, but it can very easily happen if you are not careful. If you prefer, you can try to use the ship's MARS ship-to-shore radio system for relatively inexpensive, at-sea telephone calls.

Class easy messages and Western Union telegrams, a short means of communication, are rapidly being overtaken by USOGrams and e-mail and are best suited for "alerting notice" of a problem or quasi-emergency. If you are having irritating problems and need to talk with your spouse, this method (which can be arranged through the command's radio personnel) is fairly inexpensive and almost instantaneous, and can alert your spouse to an issue requiring communication or guidance. Your message should be short, and keep in mind that it will be read by many personnel on the ship. Most units require your sailor to clear the message with the chain of command for security reasons. You can send a message through Western Union. From the ship or station, it is arranged through the radio center.

USOGrams are a good deal—relatively cheap and rapidly delivered. They are essentially a quicker means of sending a letter (which can take up to two weeks; a USOGram is usually in your sailor's hands in about two days). Like the class easy message or telegram, it will be read by others, so don't discuss anything you don't want known publicly.

Different ships, squadrons, and stations have varying policies on e-mail, so check with the command ombudsman, but it can be a terrific and rapid way to maintain connectivity at relatively low cost. Don't hesitate to explore this option, which allows you to use your computer at home to "reach out and touch" your spouse's ship, squadron, or station—generally through the command's supply center. If permitted, it can be a superb means of connection. A word of caution, however: e-mail is so convenient and instantaneous that it has been known to start up the rumor mill by allowing inaccurate or unverified information to spread rapidly. Don't add to this problem—remember that a rumor is just that until there is official confirmation by the CO, XO, command master chief (or their spouses), or the command ombudsman.

In the end, though, despite the many and new ways to contact your sailor, there is nothing like a handwritten letter. Next to a telephone call, this is the most personal, intimate, and romantic means of communication. It is completely private and permits the widest expression of thought, and you don't need to hold back on details. I would recommend trying—as much as possible—to be upbeat and positive in your letters. Obviously you should not hesitate to lay out problems or concerns; but try to keep focused on things that can be fixed and advice you really need, and let most of the letter be devoted to how much you miss your sailor and are looking forward to seeing him or her soon. Above all, keep those letters coming, even if they are just a few lines written before going to bed at night, and remember that the best letters have photos in them.

There is a special way to "communicate"—and maintain connectivity— with your spouse that is always welcome: care packages. This is a wonderful way to show your sailor that he or she is foremost in your mind. Receiving a package with treats packed in it, especially items that are hard to find overseas or while at sea, is something every sailor looks forward to. Some good choices might include favorite magazines, special candy or snack items, photos, stationery and writing instruments (perhaps as a subtle hint), hometown newspapers, articles or clippings pertaining to hobbies or locations, travel information on upcoming ports, books your sailor will love, the children's photos and their school projects (including pictures drawn by them), computer programs, videotapes of the family, cassette tapes with the children talking or telling stories— the list is as long and as personal as you can make it. But avoid anything perishable, and remember that cookies usually end up as crumbs by the time they arrive. And obviously no liquor, aerosols, explosives, or fireworks can be included.

Delivery of a care package can take a good bit longer than normal letters—from three to eight weeks—so send it early if time is important. Wrap the package carefully and put clear tape over the printed address to prevent smearing or smudging. Also, enclose a card with the delivery address inside the package. In the end, when sending a care package, it is really the thought that counts.

Children and Their Needs

Life for navy kids is challenging.

First, there is the separation from their parent. It is difficult for children to understand why Mom or Dad must spend so many nights away from home, and especially so many at one time. While they may have many friends whose mothers or fathers occasionally go on business trips, there is nothing to compare with the hurt and loss of a parent going on a long cruise. Even when they grow up with it from their earliest years, it still does not make sense in a child's mind.

Second, there is the upset and confusion over moving so often. Many navy families move every two years on average. While the navy is trying to address this significant family (and child) stress factor, there will still be far more moves in the average navy junior's life than in the lives of any of his or her peers. Moving, while challenging and occasionally difficult for adults, is often traumatic for children. This is especially true starting about ten years of age and up, when the preadolescent and the adolescent years trigger significant hormonal flows that cause emotions and feelings to be magnified. Without the coping skills that gradually develop later in life, sudden breaks in routines, schools, and—above all—friendships can be devastating.

Third, children often become concerned that Mom or Dad is in physical danger during long cruises. This is occasionally a realistic concern—as in combat or near-combat situations—but more often it results from the perception that the parent is under way in a huge sea on such a small "boat," or flying a very small, fast airplane or helicopter way up in an unforgiving sky. Such perceptions can be validated in their minds when they see images on television of planes crashing or ships running aground. Although parents can help allay these fears, they can nevertheless be very real to children, especially younger ones.

How do you deal with all of this? We will start by examining the concerns of the parents, then focus on symptoms observed in the children themselves.

For your sailor, there will be worries about losing touch with the children and missing their growth and development over a period of months, concern about being unrecognized upon return, and feelings of guilt about being a "bad" parent. As the navy spouse, you probably will be more concerned about pragmatic issues such as how to deal with the heavier workload of being a single parent, your ability to maintain discipline, and how to help ease the pain you sense your children will feel.

As for the children, they will experience some of the feelings suffered by children of divorce. These feelings may be manifested as guilt (Was it something I did that made Daddy go away?) or confusion (Why does Mommy have to go to sea?). They may result in anger, bitterness, or real fear. The following are some possible symptoms you might observe in your child when your spouse goes on deployment.

In the very young:

> clinging to favorite toys or blankets
> crying or relationship changes with friends
> hitting, shyness, eating difficulties

In older children:

> illness, stomachaches, irritation, problems in school with grades
> low self-esteem, sudden anger, loss of interest in friends or sports

This is not a pretty picture. What can you do to help your children during deployments? Fortunately, quite a bit, and while none of the ideas below can completely make the situation better, they can help your children understand and cope.

Your sailor is the most important part of the equation. First, make sure you and your sailor explain what is happening and why to the children. Be open and honest, talking face-to-face with the children, at least two months before a long cruise. Don't overdramatize dangers, adventures, or the pain of separation. Your children generally will take their cue from you on how to accept the coming separation. Try to cover the bad things—including missed holidays and birthdays—openly and forthrightly.

During your sailor's final months in port, he or she must work hard to bond emotionally with the children. Remember that younger children (under ten) have short attention spans and respond best to high-quality time together. Also, be sure to take the children to the ship or submarine to show them where Mom or Dad works, sleeps, showers, and eats. This will help them visualize your sailor as safe and well cared for.

It is also a good idea to let the children help your spouse pack. Have your sailor and the children exchange personal items before the cruise— a foreign coin or lucky token, for example—and let the children pick something from the seabag to keep during the cruise as a reminder that Mom or Dad will be home soon enough. Work with the children to make a calendar on which they can mark off days during the cruise, demonstrating to them that it is a finite amount of time everyone must face together. As your spouse's return nears, younger children might enjoy making a paper chain and ripping off a link each day until your sailor gets back.

Your spouse must work hard to keep separate and loving channels of communication open with the children during a cruise. At each port he or she should pick up a small but distinct gift, token, or postcard for each child. Each item should be mailed separately to each child—there is nothing more exciting for a child than a letter or package, especially one from a parent who is deployed. A nice touch is to include cassettes with recordings of your spouse reading books, telling stories about the ports visited, or just talking. Have your spouse enclose a self-addressed, stamped envelope and ask the child to mail back a picture of the house or a pet, or a favorite small item.

In the meantime, you should be working hard to maintain a warm, disciplined, and well-organized life for your children. Assume the disciplinarian role even before your sailor leaves on deployment, and work with your children to take over the chores your sailor normally does. Let them help pick out items for a gift box or care package for your sailor.

During any deployment, the most important thing for your child is constant reassurance that Mom or Dad is coming home soon, that your sailor misses the family very much, and that love and support are available and plentiful in the home. Spread out maps that show where your sailor is cruising, giving your children a fun geography lesson as you assure them of Mom or Dad's imminent return. And remember to keep plenty of photos of your sailor all over the house.

A Special Challenge: Dad at Sea When the Baby Is Born

There really is no good news here. Sailors whose wives are due to give birth during a cruise will, in all likelihood, miss the blessed arrival. Of my two children, my husband got back for one (barely) and missed the other. The problem is the uncertainty of the delivery date, which thus generally precludes obtaining leave to come home on time.

Many ships and commands will try to work out a means for leave after the birth, but equally likely, Dad will see the baby for the first time when the ship returns from a cruise, when the newcomer may already be four or five months of age. Childbirth, unless it involves life-threatening complications for mother or baby, does not qualify for emergency leave. Occasionally, if the birth is coming up at the very beginning or end of cruise, a temporary duty arrangement can be worked out with the command where the father is left in port for a few weeks or sent home early—but such a scenario is rare. It never hurts to ask, however, and most commands will look at each situation on a case-by-case basis. Factors considered in the decision-making process include the criticality of what the father does on the ship, the situation at home, the schedule of the deploying unit, and so forth.

Let's look at how the parties involved react in a situation where you, a navy wife, have just given birth, and your sailor is unable to make it home. Obviously, there are challenges for both parents, although, let's face it, *you* are doing all the real work. First, you are tired. If you have other children, you have to figure out how to take care of them (family, friends, and shipmates' spouses are the answer here). You may also experience postpartum depression, especially with your husband gone and perhaps not coming home for months. Once the initial flurry of activity is sorted out, and the baby is home and in a routine, it is time to work through those feelings with your husband—via writing letters, keeping a diary, making video- and audiotapes of the baby, taking plenty of pictures and annotating them—all in an effort to establish connectivity between Dad (while he is out at sea) and the baby back home. Everything becomes much easier when your husband finally comes home. And what a homecoming it will be.

On the other side of the coin, your husband will experience some mixed emotions. First, there is a sense of guilt at missing the big event and not being there to help bring the baby home, get established, and take care of the other children. Second, he will also feel very proud and will want to show photos, hand out cigars, and accept the

This happy sailor is meeting his baby girl for the first time. U.S. Naval Institute collection.

congratulations of his shipmates. Third, he will be relieved that everything is all right. Worry is part of the process for any father, perhaps
more than you realize. Finally, he will experience a little anxiety about
how he will fit into the newly expanded household.

Remember, if you are in a situation like this, as always, communication is the key. Be honest and express your feelings, and try always to
focus on the positive side. Friends can help keep homecoming anxiety
in perspective. And those with more experience in the navy know that
being separated from a husband at a time like this is not that uncommon; whenever a medium-size destroyer with a crew of three hundred
returns from a six-month deployment, there are usually several mothers on the pier holding new babies whose fathers will see them for the
first time. Seek out new mothers in the command in the same situation,
as well as those who have been through it before. You will find you are
not alone.

Separation and Reunion

Deployments are a unique challenge for any navy couple, and you may feel at times like you are the first person in the world to experience the broad spectrum of feelings that come with it. The good news is that many navy spouses have been through the same thing, and the emotions are actually fairly predictable. Let's go through the basic pattern.

During the predeployment phase, about two months before the cruise, you will probably feel some disbelief—it is too painful to think about. You may also feel anger, or you may (consciously or unconsciously) look for things to get angry about, because it is easier to say good-bye to someone with whom you are angry; likewise, you may feel some guilt for wishing your spouse would just get out on cruise and get it over with. Another common reaction is fear, as you question whether you will be able to handle everything on your own.

The first thing you must do in dealing with these emotions is communicate with your spouse. Share your feelings, and accept and try to understand what he or she is feeling as well. Try to spend plenty of time together, and—this is very important—make the practical preparations for the separation. The checklist at the end of this chapter should be very helpful in this regard.

During the first few days of the deployment itself, you may feel an odd sense of relief. This is because, for the first time in a long while, you are looking forward to something (your spouse's return) instead of dreading something (the departure). You may also feel somewhat anxious about how things will go at home, and eventually you may become frustrated at being left alone.

Remember, there are many support systems available to you—from the command's family support group, to your church, to friends and family. Take advantage of them all, and don't be afraid to enjoy yourself. Re-read chapter 5 (on "Having Fun") of this book, and talk to other spouses to find out what they are doing. You can also alleviate your loneliness by writing and communicating with your spouse, keeping physically fit, and focusing on all the good things you have going for you at home.

When your spouse finally returns, you may be surprised at the array of emotions you experience. Naturally, there is the simple pleasure of seeing your sailor again, but you may also have some nervous feelings about your sailor's acceptance of the situation at home and how to put everything back together "like it was."

Accept the fact that things have changed somewhat for both of you over six months. This is not a bad thing, but it does mean that you should both be prepared for some negotiating. Questions about cars,

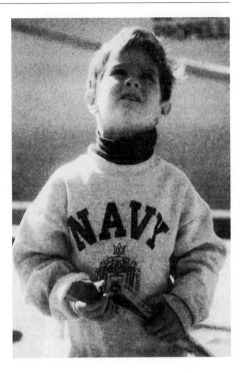

*Gift in hand, this boy is eagerly
waiting for Mom to disembark
after a six-month deployment.
U.S. Naval Institute collection.*

checkbooks, children, and household routines may come up. Both of
you should take it slow and easy; you will find it normally takes a month
or so before everyone readjusts to living together again. The NFSC has
several excellent pamphlets on reunion issues, and most commands will
sponsor a discussion of the situation as the return nears. Take advantage
of these opportunities. Each of you will have had a different reaction
to the deployment, and the intensity of new feelings may surprise you
both. The key is to celebrate the strength you both have found in your
separation, and simply enjoy being together again.

The Value of Challenge

What truly matters in life is not whether you succeed or fail at everything that comes your way, but rather how you rise to meet the inevitable challenges. And being a navy spouse will give you an opportunity to live a life full of excitement and challenge. You will have a
chance—as few others do—to face and overcome unique obstacles. Deployments, separations, moving—there will always be daunting moments. But when you do the best you can in every situation, taking ad-

vantage of the resources available and driving at the problems with energy and enthusiasm, you will overcome the challenges and succeed.

Deployment Checklist

Finances

Include amounts in the at-home spouse's budget for

> utility bills
> rent or mortgage
> monthly living expenses
> monthly payments to creditors
> savings
> once-a-year expenses that may occur during deployment, such as insurance bills

Include amounts in the deploying sailor's budget for

> port visits
> long-distance telephone calls
> gifts and souvenir purchases

Include amounts for possible income changes, including

> sea pay
> family separation allowance
> rate changes or promotions while deployed
> reenlistment or other bonuses paid while deployed

Banking Decisions

> sign up for direct deposit if not already done
> establish a means to separate funding lines, such as separate checking accounts to ease confusion over who is writing checks and when they are written, or separate payments
> set credit limits for each spouse, or decide who will be using credit cards during deployment
> make sure checking and savings accounts are in the same bank, so funds can easily be transferred

Allotments

Review your financial situation to see if your need to establish any additional allotments.

"D" Dependent allotment
"B" Bond allotment
"C" Contribution allotment
"H" Home allotment
"S" Savings allotment
"I" Insurance allotment

Vehicles

complete regular vehicle maintenance before deployment
know where vehicle insurance, tags, and inspection stickers are
   located, and what will expire during deployment and how to
   renew
keep the name of a trusted mechanic/repair garage handy
know the correct type of battery, tires, oil; maintain basic
   knowledge of the vehicle

Emergency Plans

try to save at least one month's pay in a savings account to use
   in case of emergency
give a family member your sailor's complete and official mailing address, social security number, and ombudsman's telephone number
be aware of services available through the NFSC and NMRCS
teach children how to contact the American Red Cross in case
   of emergency

Legal

ensure your command's personnel office checks page two of
   your sailor's service record to make sure the correct information is listed
make sure the correct beneficiary is listed on your sailor's SGLI
   paperwork
visit the base legal office to have a will drawn up for both you
   and your sailor
decide whether or not you need a power of attorney; visit base
   legal for advice and to have this done
have a special medical power of attorney drafted for child care
   providers, if applicable
know the location of important documents such as wills, mar-

riage and birth certificates, and insurance policies (your sailor
should know this too)

check expiration dates on family members' ID cards and
arrange for obtaining new cards if necessary

verify DEERS enrollment for family members; call 1-800-538-
9552 to confirm enrollment

Home/Apartment

know what to do or who to call if something in your home
breaks; have a list with a trusted plumber, electrician, and
home repairperson

give your home a security check inside and out; make sure all
door and window locks work

test all smoke and CO_2 alarms; install new batteries

know the process for moving your household goods

review your homeowner's and renters' insurance policies

know where the master turn-offs are for water, gas, and
electricity

Communication

agree on how often you will write to each other and discuss
what information you want to share

number your letters throughout the deployment (both of you
should do this)

plan in advance for frequency and length of telephone
calls

plan for ways to remain connected with relatives; decide who
will write and/or send birthday gifts to parents

duplicate calendars marked with special events, birthdays,
school and community activities; use calendars for the
homecoming countdown

have photos taken of you and your sailor together and another
of your sailor alone

recognize your feelings; talk about them with your sailor

develop a list of items your sailor wants and needs in care packages, including magazines, local newspapers, grooming
items, and favorite foods

order flowers in advance for special occasions

give your sailor a lucky keepsake for the cruise

include children in discussions on where and why their parent
is going and when returning

set short-term goals to accomplish during the deployment (both of you should do this)

keep current on the navy community at home by reading the base newspaper, and let your sailor know what is going on

know the ship's Careline number and the ombudsman's number; keep them on the refrigerator

send taped messages to each other; be romantic and write love letters—you will never have a better chance

Parenting

prepare children for deployment by taking them to the ship; show them where your sailor will be, including the bunk, mess decks or wardroom, and work spaces

learn the typical reactions children have when a parent deploys by attending a parent-child deployment program, reading, or talking with NFSC staff, the ombudsman, or experienced parents

let your children share in preparations for the homecoming

9
Steady Steaming and Making Port

Twilight and evening bell,
And after that the dark!
And may there be no sadness of farewell,
When I embark.
> "Crossing the Bar"
> Alfred Lord Tennyson

Perhaps the most important decision you and your spouse will make together is whether to continue your sailor's navy career. There are two decision points you will face: the end of obligated service, and retirement eligibility. In this chapter, we will examine some of the factors you should consider when deciding whether to remain in the navy or whether to move on, as well as some of the resources available to help you before, during, and after your decision.

Navy Careers and the End of Obligated Service

When your spouse joined the navy, he or she might have enlisted or been commissioned with the idea of serving a limited time, then moving on to the civilian world. Enlisted sailors sign contracts that specify the minimum amount of time they must serve; the conclusion of that period is called their end of active obligated service, or EAOS. Officers, on the other hand, serve at the pleasure of the president. They are free to submit a resignation—a request to depart the service—but certain restrictions apply. Generally, officers incur a period of obligated service upon their commissioning (about five years, depending on source program and career field), after attending schools or war college, or upon accepting a large bonus in certain specialties. If one of those factors does not apply, the officer can submit a resignation, which will generally be approved, and move on.

This career decision should be based on many factors. Although it may seem negative, a good approach is to examine a list of the "typical" reasons sailors leave the navy. Think about how you and your spouse feel about each of these factors, which are discussed in the next section. Then work through the benefits of remaining, and how they measure up against the negatives. Draw up a "benefits and challenges" list and assign weight to each of the factors. Don't make it too technical; these types of decisions, in the end, are intuitive rather than analytical. But making a list will help you and your spouse focus on the decision at hand and will probably give you solid clues about which way to go.

The Challenges

Certainly the first and most frequently cited reason for leaving the navy at the end of obligated service is simple and painful: *family separation.* No one who is happily married likes to deal with the reality of spending weeks or months away from family and friends. But like anything else, and as we have discussed in this book, there are many resources and ways to help you cope with the pain of family separation. And you will be rotated ashore for plenty of good family time, generally between sea duty tours. Yet this is undeniably a major negative factor in navy life, and a very real consideration in deciding whether or not to remain in the navy for a full career.

Pay and benefits is another factor to consider. This is a very subjective area, with some people quite satisfied with their navy pay and others believing they could earn more as civilians. A good way to approach this factor is to try to assess honestly how much money your sailor could make as a civilian. This will vary, of course, depending on education, skills, intelligence, location, and so forth. A midgrade officer with an advanced engineering degree from the naval postgraduate school probably could quickly surpass his or her navy earnings. On the other hand, a first class petty officer with skills oriented toward deck operations may feel appropriately compensated. Remember that a good-sized chunk of your spouse's pay is not taxed, which means about 20–30 percent more in your pocket. You also receive medical benefits, commissary and exchange privileges, access to recreational facilities, and other benefits that are difficult to "price out." You can have your sailor check with the unit's disbursing officer for an assessment of "equivalent pay," which will put a price on some of these factors. You may be surprised what your navy compensation package is worth compared to civilian pay scales.

Frequent moves are something else to think about. While many families enjoy this aspect of military life, others find it frustrating to be forced to move every two to three years. The need for you, your children, and even your pets to reorder your lives completely—from jobs, to schools, to shopping, to veterinarians—is very demanding. It has very real financial consequences in terms of spousal employment and moving costs that are typically not fully compensated. Moving can also be very hard on children, especially as they struggle to make new friends every couple of years. I remember my own childhood as being very challenging in that regard, although it has made me a confident and friendly person as a result. In any event, this is again a very personal factor that affects people differently. Additionally, be aware that the navy is attempting to keep people in the same geographic area, moving from ship to shore and back to sea duty again without having to leave. This idea is being successfully pursued in the navy's "megaports" of Norfolk and San Diego in particular.

Risk is a factor that is difficult to categorize but is sometimes considered. Let's face it, there are no other jobs—with the possible exception of urban police and fire officers—where the worker faces the real possibility of violence and danger on a daily basis. This is true most obviously in combat situations, but it is also a factor in regular peacetime training, especially for those involved in flying or who work on aircraft carriers.

Downsizing is a negative that was associated with the military. Since the end of the Cold War, the military has been significantly cut in size, with the navy reducing the number of its ships from nearly six hundred at its Cold War peak to about three hundred today. In the mid-1990s, these cuts forced people to leave the navy when they did not choose to. Today, however, the navy is fairly stable and further significant downsizing is unlikely, given enduring U.S. security concerns and needs (Persian Gulf, Korean peninsula, global stability, regional presence, strategic weapons) in the post–Cold War world.

The *rigid command structure* of the military is another area that can be troublesome to people. Certain types of personalities are less suited to military life than others, and while your sailor may do very well, he or she may not be happy in a hierarchical, highly structured system like the military. This is a very personal factor to consider, and the best approach is simply to ask your spouse and yourself if you are happy in the military environment, or if something about it—from the uniforms to the rank structure—bothers you for one reason or another. It is perfectly all right to feel that you and your spouse would rather be in the civilian world, where there is generally more flexibility in the workplace. Don't be naive, however: just because employees don't wear uniforms with rank designations on their sleeves at IBM, for example, does not mean they are not largely hierarchical in their approach. If your sailor leaves the military because of its rigid structure, you need to focus the family employment search on more unstructured industries altogether.

Long hours must be mentioned in any discussion about navy life. At sea, the typical workday is over sixteen hours, generally seven days per week. Even ashore, the hours can be very long, running from 7:00 A.M. quarters to some occasional late nights preparing for inspections. And there is no overtime paid. This is a serious and legitimate complaint about the navy, and the only real defense for this is that it is the price you pay for the right to serve—this is why it is called the service. On top of the long hours, your sailor will stand some duty nights onboard the ship, perhaps as many as one in four. This is a demanding aspect of navy life that is not typical of the civilian sector, outside of police, fire fighters, and physicians, and it is a factor you should consider carefully.

Finally, there are *personal reasons* for wanting to leave the navy. Some examples might be aging parents who need full-time support; a family business or farm to take over; or a desire to do something unrelated to the military, such as teaching elementary school. You should close out your list with any personal reasons, and then consider all of the factors as you and your spouse contemplate remaining with or leaving the navy.

The Benefits

There are, fortunately, many good reasons to stay in the navy. Let's discuss a few key ones.

Great coworkers are at the top of many people's lists for staying in the navy. You will very seldom find an organization that has such quality, motivated, well-educated, and positive people. Naturally, there are a few difficult folks, just as there are in any job, but by and large the navy population is honest, decent, adventurous, and friendly. And the day-to-day support from fellow sailors counts for quite a bit in terms of job satisfaction.

Adventure and travel is another—as well as the simplest—key factor that keeps people in the service. There simply are not many jobs where you launch airplanes from the deck of a one-hundred-thousand-ton ship, let alone fly them off; or have the chance to bring a gas-turbine-powered destroyer into a dock with high winds blowing; or launch Tomahawk missiles in retaliation of terrorist attacks; or sail a nuclear submarine under the polar ice. Your sailor (and probably you as well) will travel throughout the world and the United States in the course of your naval career. "Sure beats working for a living," as my husband often says.

Educational opportunity is higher in the armed services, and particularly in the navy, than just about anywhere else. Throughout your sailor's time in the navy, he or she will receive training and education in virtually every area—technical, leadership, management—at no cost. Additionally, the navy is a huge supporter of after-hours education, and works hard to make college education available and affordable through a wide variety of programs. There are also schools that range from the Naval War

College to welding classes. The average officer spends over 20 percent of his or her career attending schools, for example, and this includes opportunities to obtain a master's degree fully funded at the navy's expense. Such opportunities are likewise reflected at the enlisted level as well.

The solid *retirement plan* in the navy is a plus. It is still the only program that is fully and completely backed by the U.S. government and permits retirement with a significant stipend (50 percent of base pay) at the twenty-year point. Enlisted people can put in twenty years and walk away from the service with a nice pension at only thirty-seven years of age; this leaves plenty of time for a second career, with a permanent fallback position available to them.

An *honest and stable employer* is another benefit of serving in the navy. The U.S. government is not in imminent danger of collapsing anytime soon, and despite recent cuts, there will always be a need for a U.S. Navy to defend our international interests and protect our thousands of miles of coastlines.

The *respect and prestige* afforded to members of the navy is a real and valuable benefit of serving. Your fellow citizens will respect what your sailor does, and they will empathize with your sacrifices as a navy spouse as well. You will be a real part of our nation's defense, and your patriotism and devotion to country will be satisfying to you and your sailor every day. Everyone should be proud of the work they do, and in the navy, you will always feel a part of an important mission that matters to your country very much.

Advancement and recognition are related to respect and prestige, and can be a very important factor for your sailor. The opportunity to advance based on merit and fair promotion boards, as well as the opportunity to receive medals and other formal recognition, is a rewarding element of a navy career. Your sailor could spend a long time in many civilian jobs without receiving any recognition or advancement other than a paycheck, and over a matter of years such lack of recognition can be disturbing to some people. The navy, on the other hand, is oriented toward moving people up and ensuring that hard work is fairly rewarded. Don't underestimate this factor as a source of pleasure and satisfaction in your family's life.

Deciding

Armed with the two lists above—the challenges and the benefits—you and your sailor should be able to sit down and individually evaluate your personal situation in terms of whether to stay or depart at the end of obligated service.

There are several important sources of help available to you as you make this important decision. First and foremost are the command's career counselors. These individuals are specially trained to help advise on these types of decisions, although they are certainly biased in favor of keeping your spouse in the navy. As a result, they are best employed as a source of data. The Bureau of Naval Personnel's Center for Career Development also has information and can be approached through the command career counselor.

A third, and generally less biased, source of information and advice can be found in your sailor's chain of command. For officers, discussing options with the next senior in the chair, as well as with the CO and XO, is a good idea. Caution your sailor not to come across as negative or whining; if you and your spouse decide to stay in the navy, he or she will want to maintain a good reputation in the command. If your spouse approaches the decision honestly and openly, he or she will almost always receive commensurately honest and open advice from the chain of command. Everyone in the navy goes through the process of deciding to stay in or get out, and your sailor's chain of command will empathize and try and direct him or her in the right direction.

You and your spouse can also turn to peers who have themselves recently faced the same decisions. Try to find a couple who decided to stay in and one who decided to get out. You may be surprised at what you hear, both pro and con, and they may have considered some factor you and your sailor have not.

Of course, there is always the NFSC, which can be a good source of general information. They provide transition seminars that have employment and benefit information, and the counselors are quite familiar with the entire process of staying in or getting out themselves. Drop by and see the people there to discuss upcoming seminars, and they will be able to point you and your spouse to appropriate resources.

Finally, don't forget to check the LIFELines web site, which also has a wide-range of information available.

Retirement

Naturally, deciding to retire is very different from deciding to leave at the end of obligated service. If the two of you are considering retirement, presumably you have enjoyed the navy enough to "hang in there" throughout two decades of service. You may now be thinking about leaving for a variety of reasons, including better opportunities, weariness of moving and family separation, a desire to try something new, and the cost benefit (after all, following twenty years of service, you could draw your pension for *not* working, so the decision to remain on active duty is often called "working for half-pay" as a joke).

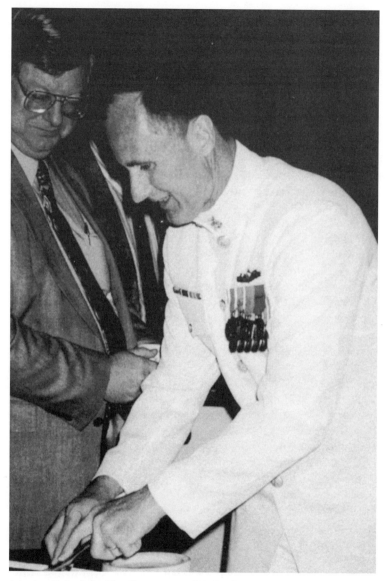

A master chief enjoying his retirement party. U.S. Naval Institute collection.

Whatever your reasons for considering retirement, you should still approach the decision somewhat like you would at the end of obligated service. Begin by making a list of pros and cons, using as a baseline the lists above. Then consider the following additional factors that pertain when you are retirement eligible.

Opportunity costs. This simply means that after twenty years, you could be drawing 50 percent of your base pay without doing any work for the navy. So if you continue to work for the navy, your salary is worth, in some senses, far less. Instead of staying in the navy, you could be drawing the retirement checks and working for full pay at another job, generally for at least as much money as you were making in the navy. Thus there are opportunity costs in remaining on active duty after twenty years.

Upward mobility (or the lack of it). After twenty years, most people in the navy are pretty close to "topping out." The vast majority of individuals will not go beyond commander (O-5) as officers, or senior chief petty officer (E-8) as enlisted. Even moving that far is quite an achievement in today's smaller navy. So sailors need to evaluate honestly where they are in the pattern and whether or not (a) they are at the top of their promotability; and (b) whether it matters to them. Some people are quite happy to continue moving along horizontally, doing important and effective work, and working toward full thirty-year retirement. Others, on the other hand, want to depart the navy the moment they perceive they are not moving up the "corporate" ladder. In either case, the key is that your sailor be honest about expectations and realities. A friend of mine used to say, "In the end, the navy will break your heart," meaning that sooner or later almost everyone is denied a promotion or advancement, even the CNO who fails to "make the cut" for Chairman of the Joint Chiefs of Staff. Being realistic about where your spouse is career wise will help you keep your perspective and make your decisions accordingly.

Second career. Perhaps the most important aspect of the retirement decision is your sailor's approach to this factor. Again, this is very personal and subjective. Some retired navy people want to shoot for another "navy-like" experience—a full, challenging, and exciting twenty- to thirty-year run through life. Such folks may move on to be investment bankers, lawyers, contractors, and so on. Others want something low-key and life-style friendly, perhaps teaching at an elementary school or running a small bait shop (my husband's choice). Still others are not interested in a second career at all and would prefer to spend time golfing or fishing. Obviously, if your sailor wants another challenging and upwardly mobile career, the right moment to get out is sooner rather than later. While this will mean less retirement pay (he or she will draw the minimum 50 percent of base pay), it does mean more years as a civilian and a younger start at a second career. If your spouse is interested in a middle option, he or she could get out around the twenty-six-year point. This will maximize retirement pay versus time remaining to work as a civilian. If full retirement after the navy is the goal (and if your finances will support it), the right path may be a thirty-year run with the navy, which will give your family the top end of the retirement package, conceivably up to 75 percent of base pay. And a second career can still be a viable option.

Retirement Considerations

If you and your spouse make the decision to retire, there is a whole new world of information with which you will need to be acquainted before the actual event.

The first thing to do is to assemble the references. A good general-purpose book on the subject is *Retiring from Military Service,* written by K. C. Jacobsen and published by the U.S. Naval Institute. This well-written, common-sense guide covers such topics as the Survivors' Benefit Plan (the decision to receive less retired pay in order to guarantee it to survivors—generally you, the spouse—after the retiree passes on); medical benefits, which change somewhat after retirement, although medical care remains guaranteed; educational opportunities; job searching; retirement vacations; and a wealth of other information. Another good resource is the Retired Officers Association, located at 201 N. Washington Street, Alexandria, Virginia, 22314-2529. They publish various guides, including *Marketing Yourself for a Second Career* and *Planning for Military Retirement.* Joining the association (applications are in the *Navy Times* each week) is a good idea. The navy has published a useful book entitled *Navy Guide for Retired Personnel and Their Families,* which can be found at your spouse's command. Read it from cover to cover—it is full of good advice and important facts. Finally, there are dozens of excellent books on the market about job hunting, switching careers and jobs, and surviving retirement. Pick out a few and read them with your spouse in the months before you actually leave.

An Ex–Navy Spouse?

So your spouse finally did it—left the navy. Whether it was after a single "hitch" of four years, either as an enlisted sailor or as an officer, or after a glorious forty-year career ending with flag rank as a full four-star admiral, you are now officially an ex–navy spouse. Or are you?

I suspect that you will find yourself looking back frequently on your days with the navy. I guarantee you that your spouse will. The last day he or she pulls on the uniform will be emotional, and in the years after leaving the navy, your ex-sailor will occasionally look back nostalgically on his or her days in the service. You will both tend to forget the painful separations, the constant moves, the dangerous deployments; and you will remember the good friends, the exciting travel, and the honor of serving your country. Just as your spouse will always, to some degree, find him- or herself touched by the navy, so will you. "Anchors Aweigh" will send a nostalgic shiver up your spine, and the sight of a navy man or woman swinging down the street or on a movie or television screen will make you sigh and remember the days when you were part of a great navy family.

That sweet sense of remembering is a good thing, even if you feel somewhat wistful at the same time. It is a good thing because you are recalling a time when you were younger and perhaps more free and full of the adventure of life. You knew it couldn't last forever, and it wasn't always perfect, but deep down you will admit there was something very special about being "married to the navy." My advice is to stay in touch with your navy friends—those still in the navy and those who have left— and to keep track of what is going on in the navy that was once such a big part of your life. Just as there are no ex-marines, there really are no ex–navy spouses, either. You are part of a club of women and men who have helped and supported our navy and our nation in a very special way. Be proud of your navy and your role in it for the rest of your life.

10
Standing Beside the Leader

Chant on, sail on, bear o'er the boundless blue, from me, to every sea,
This song for mariners and all their ships.

"In Cabin'd Ships at Sea"
Walt Whitman

After you have spent some time in the navy family, you may find yourself moving, alongside your spouse, into positions of more responsibility within a command. At each, you will have a better sense of the overall mission of the command, be it in a ship, submarine, shore station, aircraft squadron, SEAL unit, or any other navy activity. As your spouse's career develops, you may find yourself increasingly involved in command support activities, interacting with its leadership and helping to shape the atmosphere of the command in positive ways. In the following chapter, I have outlined a few basic thoughts about your role.

Petty Officer's Spouse

Making Petty Officer, or E-4 through E-6 in the navy is a great achievement. Your spouse has been in the navy two years to twenty years, so this rating can represent a number of people. The role of a petty officer in the navy is to provide leadership to small groups of sailors organized in a work center or other subset of the overall command. Your spouse, especially a more senior E-6 petty officer, will play a significant leadership role in his or her unit. For instance, your spouse may provide technical advice on mission accomplishment; serve as a sponsor for newly arrived junior sailors; participate on support committees, such as the welfare and recreation, menu review, and family support committees; or give advice and leadership to young people.

As the spouse of a petty officer, your role will parallel that of your wife or husband. You may find yourself working with younger spouses, and you should feel free to do so, although you need to be careful not to be overbearing or bossy at any point. Remember, at every level in the command, as a navy spouse, you do not wear the rank or have the authority of the military. You are standing beside the leader, but you are not the leader yourself. Additionally, be careful not to give advice on a

CO and XO spouses are part of the command leadership team. Author's collection.

personal basis; rather, confine yourself to what might be termed as being "professionally supportive." Examples of ways to be supportive or helpful include the following:

> connect newly arrived spouses with the command ombudsman
> let them know how to get in touch with Family Service Center
> make sure they are added to the command telephone tree, receive the Careline telephone number, and are electronically connected to the command, if they have e-mail capability
> provide advice to the newly arrived about the local commissary as well as medical, dental, and other services
> offer ideas on child care and employment opportunities in the home port

As the spouse of a petty officer, you should strive to present a positive and upbeat opinion of the navy and the command. If you see a spouse struggling, you should encourage him or her to contact the command ombudsman, chaplain, or Family Service Center. Try to be helpful without being intrusive.

Chief Petty Officer's Spouse

Making chief petty officer is a great moment in any navy career. With greater rank and privilege comes additional responsibility for the active duty service member. This will often translate into a more considerable role for the spouse. Many chief petty officers' wives find themselves serving as command ombudsmen, chair of the family support group, and organizers of special ship committees, such as for the ship holiday parties and homecoming festivities. The ten years' or more experience that a chief petty officer's spouse has often enables them to be very knowledgeable and helpful in these tasks.

It is important to remember that these activities are all voluntary. You should undertake them because you want to and because you feel a desire to help, not because you feel obligated or—for the worst possible motivation—because you think it will help your spouse's career. The navy recognizes that today's spouses lead busy lives: most spouses work and the demands of small children can be great. You should assess your particular situation before jumping into a major commitment. A good approach is to volunteer for an activity with a restricted time frame; perhaps, you might put together the ship's Easter party or arrange some aspect of the command's homecoming. If this works well and you enjoy it, you might want to consider larger responsibilities such as a family support group office.

The most demanding role is that of ombudsman, and this should only be undertaken by a spouse with a lot of time and a real desire to do the job, plus navy experience—ten years' experience, minimum, in my mind. Ombudsmen receive formal training from the navy and help from the command, but it is still a very demanding job. You should talk it over seriously with your spouse and some of the other leadership spouses before considering to be a candidate for ombudsman. Having said that, it is a rewarding experience to be able to help many other navy spouses.

Division Officer and Department Head Spouse

Most navy commands are broken into a structure of divisions led by junior officers, O-1 through O-3. These in turn are part of larger departments led by O-3s and O-4s, and on the larger ships and installations by O-5s. At each of these levels, you will find the opportunity to be involved in command-wide spouse activity.

As a division officer's spouse, you will be involved with the ship's support group, with spouses of other wardroom officers, and possibly with spouses in the division. Division officer spouses are encouraged to be involved in planning ship social functions, such as holiday parties, Halloween parades, spring picnics, summer beach days, or trips to an amusement park. Given your spouse's leadership role in the command, you are a logical candidate to work on some of these activities. Again, as for any other spouse, there is no obligation. Your education, background, and personal situation should dictate whether this makes sense for you. Most commands have informal gatherings of the wardroom spouses, perhaps potluck dinners while the command is deployed or on a spouse's night out. If your wardroom holds these on a rotating basis, you should consider hosting one yourself. While not a navy requirement, there is, of course, a certain social obligation that if you are accepting the hospitality of others you should reciprocate at some point. Review our earlier chapter on entertaining and don't feel intimidated that you must do something fancy just because someone else did. A pizza and beer party is just fine, if that's what feels right for you. Generally speaking, wardroom spouse functions are casual and purely social.

At the department head level, you are approaching leadership involvement at a broad level in the command. Department heads can have in excess of a hundred sailors working for them, so you will observe many situations involving spouses. You may find yourself called by a spouse, especially while the command is deployed, with questions or problems. You should be a conduit for information, not a problem solver. Refer any department spouse who needs help to the command ombudsman or the command master chief. The regional chaplain can also be helpful if you cannot contact either command representative and the problem is immediate. Make sure you keep the service spouse informed by using e-mail or Imarsat sailor telephone, as necessary. In addition, it is always a good idea to let the CO's or XO's spouses know about any situations that arise. The calls you receive may range from relatively simple car breakdowns to child-care challenges. Always be polite and try to be of assistance. Remember that you were once a young spouse starting out, and it is hoped that you were able to turn to others with longer navy experience to receive good ideas and advice. As always, remember your efforts are as a volunteer and that in the end you aren't wearing any rank. Nonetheless, people will think of you as being "senior" and "experienced," and you should do your best to provide them with good advice and involve command professionals—primarily, the ombudsman—early.

Commanding Officer and Executive Officer Spouses

I think the best and most succinct advice I can give comes from a speech I gave at the October 2000 East Coast CO and XO Spouses' Conference in Norfolk, Virginia. The following excerpt summarizes one approach to being the spouse of either a CO or an XO, the two senior leadership positions in the command. I'd like to emphasize one more time that it is your spouse, *not you,* who wears the rank in the navy. As a CO's or XO's spouse, it is easy to be caught up in the position and become domineering. Remember, you are there to assist and in effect to serve, not the other way around. Keep "service to the crew" as your guiding principle, and you'll be just fine.

Standing Beside the Leader

I am very glad to be here today, and I hope what I have to say will be helpful as each of you head off to new challenges and experiences as spouses of commanding officers and executive officers. Certainly the events of the past week and the incredible courage of the sailors and families of the USS *Cole* should inspire all of us to underscore how important and challenging a role our navy serves in the world today. I know each one of us can identify with the families of *Cole,* and our thoughts and prayers are with them this week.

I very clearly remember sitting right where you are some years ago and wondering what it would be like to be an XO's spouse—in my case, Jim served on an Aegis cruiser in Long Beach, California—or as a CO's spouse, as when Jim had a command on the *Barry* here in Norfolk. Conferences like these are helpful in terms of getting people together to talk about issues, and I want to start by saying that there are no right answers to most of the questions we'll be discussing over the course of this conference. So much depends on your particular circumstances, your intuition, and your personality—as well as your spouse's.

I like to think that experience does count, and it is hoped that, as a group, we can share those experiences in a productive way in order to help each of us work through the challenges of life in the navy and the CO or XO spouse role.

. . .

Let me address the question of how involved you should be in your role as the CO or XO spouse. I think the answer is that you should be as involved as you can comfortably be, based on your own situation, experience, and personality.

Start by asking yourself, What can I offer? Not everyone has experience, of course, and a good rule of thumb is to think about how long you've been associated with the navy. If you and your spouse have been married and with the navy for more than five years, your knowledge base is higher than about 80 percent of the other spouses in the command. More than ten years puts your experience ahead of about 90 percent of them. That kind of experience is a significant asset. Additionally, if you thought that one day you would be the spouse of the CO or XO, you probably spent some time thinking about it. You might have attended conferences like today's, and you might have talked with other more experienced spouses. The bottom line is that you may not feel like an expert, but you probably have a good level of knowledge and a sense of how to work within the system to get answers.

Second, you will need to examine your own situation. Do you have small children at home? Are you working a full-time, demanding job, with after-work responsibilities? Do you have medical concerns for yourself or others in your immediate family? Do you have an exceptional family member? All of these are factors you should consider before deciding what your level of commitment and involvement should be.

Third, you should think about your own personality. This can be the hardest part for many people. Let's face it, not everyone is an accurate judge of her own character, so your spouse can be a useful gauge for assessing your qualities in a tactful way. In general, if you are a fairly calm person, reasonably well organized, and have a genuine concern for others, you will do fine. You do not have to be a combination of Mother Theresa and Bill Gates—just a normal, good-hearted person. One point to consider: if you tend to get too passionate about helping others and quickly become emotionally involved with people, you may want to be cautious about the depth of your involvement.

Armed with this self-assessment of experience, situation, and personality, you should be able to make a good judgment of the level of day-to-day involvement you want in the command. The key is not to force yourself into a situation where you overcommit and find yourself unable to follow through. On the other hand, you shouldn't use this to make excuses for not being involved because I next want to discuss the rewards of being an involved CO or XO spouse.

Essentially, these are internal rewards, which is to say they are the very best kind. These are the moments when you help direct a newly arrived spouse to a Family Service Center for good advice on finding a job or a place to live, when you work with the ombudsman to set up a spouse web site for the command, when you help pull together homecoming festivities with the command's support group chairperson. All of these are pretty nice moments. Notice, please, that in each of those examples, you are not doing everything yourself. In fact, you can consider yourself as a conductor in the orchestra support system. There are a lot of instruments in the orchestra: ombudsman, command master chief, support group leadership, Family Service Center, chain of command, the new web site LIFELines, numerous publications. Just as a conductor cannot play every instrument in the orchestra, your role is not to be the master of all that information; rather, you should be a conductor of the resources with a sense of how the music ought to sound.

Central to all of this, of course, are the spouses. Let's not forget them.

First, never start to think that you are wearing your spouse's rank, or that you are in charge of anything in the navy. I think we have all encountered a few spouses who have made this mistake and witnessed the very corrosive effect it can have on a command. Your role is to stand *beside* the leader, not *to be* the leader. Believe me, there is plenty to do in that support role, and everything you do should be a cooperative effort with your spouse.

One of the finest additions over the past couple of years is the Command Spouse Leadership Course, which provides an opportunity for navy spouses to travel to Newport and work with their partner to put together a command charter. I highly encourage you to take advantage of this, if possible, as it can make a real difference in your comfort level—particularly in the first few months in the command.

Let me next address a situation that you may encounter when you are unable to really dig in and take on the role of a fully involved CO or XO spouse. You made an honest self-assessment of your experience, situation, and personality, and with your spouse you found that being fully engaged will not be possible. Perhaps you are remaining behind at the old duty station to allow your child to complete the school year, or you have a medical issue, or a demanding job that requires travel. Now what?

This is where you and your spouse, along with the other key leadership members and their spouses, should think about identifying an alternate. I have witnessed this working quite well at every level. In one of my husband's commands, the wife of the captain remained behind in another city and, although she made a good effort to be involved, it became necessary for the XO's spouse to take the lead in many local events. This was not a problem because everyone discussed it beforehand and agreed to the alternate. I also watched a department head's spouse step forward to help in an XO spouse role when the XO was not married. I also have seen wives in major commands who did not want to be involved due to professional demands, and their role was taken over by the ombudsman. There are many ways to solve this problem, and it simply takes an open discussion, a balanced look at the command, and your personal situation.

Having said this, please remember that being a CO or XO spouse is not an "all or nothing" situation. If you can be involved a little bit, great. Just be sure you figure out who can cover when you cannot be available. Your contributions will be appreciated. In some ways, it is like endeavoring to speak a foreign language. You don't have to be fluent; rather, you get a lot of credit for the effort you make and the spirit with which you try.

I also want to talk a little about taking care of yourself. It is very easy to overcommit in today's world. We recognize this tendency to take on too much constantly, not only in ourselves but in our spouses and children as well. I think all of us can relate to the juggling of time and energy that is necessary to manage a ten-year-old child's activities today. There is a very frenetic pace to modern life that just was not imaginable when we were children, and let's face it, by taking on the CO or XO spouse role, you are taking on a considerable new commitment.

Hence, you must take care of yourself. Naturally, you will be keeping a close eye on your spouse, your children, on the command, and on your other outside commitments. It is very easy to let yourself slide to the back of the pack. The problem with doing so, of course, is that you will burn out, overcommit, and underdeliver. In the end no one—not you, not your spouse, not the command—will benefit. As a CO or XO spouse, you are running a marathon—not a sprint—and there are three good rules to bear in mind.

One, keep your sense of humor and do not take yourself too seriously. While you are dealing with important issues, do not start to think of yourself as hugely important or that the world is wondering what you are doing as the CO or XO spouse. We are all part of a far-reaching, larger world, with a lot happening. The odds are good that the future of the republic is not going to rise or fall based on the outcome of your command picnic or the turnout at the November support group meeting.

My second rule of taking care of yourself is to not take everything personally. Do not get bogged down in the personalities of the command when things do not go well for whatever reason, whether it is a problem with failing the latest inspection on a ship, an unruly support group meeting, or an ombudsman who runs off with a petty officer from another submarine. Do not let it affect your personal sense of who you are. Rise above the situation, stay steady and calm, talk to your spouse and to others in the leadership, and try to be the voice of reason—not emotion. It is easy to say and occasionally hard to do, but your cumulative life experiences—not necessarily your navy experience—should help you considerably.

Third, and perhaps of most importance, take time off when you need it. If you need a break from the schedule of the ship, tell your ombudsman or fellow leadership spouse, "I'm really busy during the next couple of weeks, can you cover?" Remember, while *this* is important and meaningful work, you have to balance a lot of priorities. Letting yourself become run down, especially while the command is deployed, is bad for the long-term. Again, think marathon, not sprint.

As a final thought, let me return to the USS *Cole* and the families today. I know the entire navy will wrap its arms around the ship and the families. Each one of us might find ourselves in a similar situation some day because this is the risk we live with every day. The key to being a CO or XO spouse in a high-stress real world situation like this remains the same. Stay close with the other members of the command leadership. Take your cue and your information from an official source, preferably directly from the CO or XO or, if they are unavailable due to the operations, from the next level in the homeport chain of command. Ensure that the occurrence of rumors is minimized by having a single, official source of information, such as the Careline. Never feel that you—or anyone in the command—is obligated to talk with the media. If for some reason you do, do not speak without professional advice from a navy public affairs officer (PAO). Stay connected with the ship but recognize that they are in an intense operational situation. Remain upbeat and positive in all of your dealings with your command family. And above all remember that as our ships, aircraft, and submarines operate around the globe, they may take risks but they also are in the world's finest navy, with a strong support system of which you all are an important part.

I want to close with a wonderful quote from Arthur Ashe, the late Wimbledon tennis champion, a man who balanced his career, his family, and his sense of service extraordinarily well within the high pressure world of professional athletics. He was speaking about his career when he said, "You are really never playing an opponent. You are playing yourself, your own high standards, and when you reach your goals, that is real joy." I like that quote because it reminds me that we are not competing with anyone else's ideal of being a CO or XO spouse, but rather, we are trying to do our best to set standards that we can realistically achieve to make the navy a better place for everyone. That, I think, is what being a CO or XO spouse is about. As you stand beside the leader, set a standard you can realistically achieve, try your best, work to make the U.S. Navy a great place to serve, and enjoy every minute.

Resources for Spouses

Two fairly recent developments of interest particularly for CO and XO spouses are the Command Spouse Leadership Course in Newport and the COMPASS course.

The Command Spouse Leadership Course in Newport is an opportunity for prospective commanding officers and their spouses to participate in a week of lectures, exercises, and team-building experiences. The course is given eighteen times during the year from Monday through Friday, and is funded by the navy under invitational orders. The course focuses on building an effective commanding officer–spouse team, and enhances team-building and communication skills, as well as personal growth. It provides the dedicated time and tools for the couple to discuss, prioritize, plan, and formulate their Command Tour Charter. The charter should reflect each of their goals and the participation expected in both the professional and personal facets of the command tour. Should your spouse be fortunate enough to be assigned to command, I highly recommend that you participate in this course. Not only will it pay great dividends during the command tour ahead, but attendees earn three hours of college credit.

COMPASS is a ten-hour, spouse-to-spouse mentoring program that was piloted in Norfolk in January 2001 and is open to all navy spouses at the larger navy bases around the U.S. Based on similar programs for army and Marine Corps spouses, the course is free—with babysitting provided—and is sponsored by the Naval Services' FamilyLine, formerly the Navy Wifeline Association. Trained navy spouses, acting as volunteer mentors, teach the program, which covers all aspects of the navy lifestyle, including the navy's mission, history, customs and traditions, rights and benefits, pay, deployments and relocations, interpersonal communication, and investment in self and community. It is hoped that this course will be expanded and be available in your homeport. Check with the local Family Service Center to see if it is currently available where you are stationed or if the NFSC can suggest other courses that provide similar information. I recommend all our navy spouses take the course, so they can help others in our expanded navy family.

A Concluding Thought

There are many opportunities for you to volunteer in your spouse's command; it is not an "all or nothing" proposition. Try getting involved at a trial level and see how it feels. The rewards are plenty as you stand beside a leader in the command and are very much a part of the diverse set of experiences that make the navy so special.

A Final Note

It is an important rule, written in a book somewhere, that everything should end with a poem.

This wonderful poem was published in 1935 by Roberta Burke. "Bobbie" Burke spent over seventy years at the side of one of the navy's great twentieth-century heroes, Adm. Arleigh Burke, who was chief of naval operations for a record six years and a World War II destroyer commodore. Admiral Burke died on 1 January 1996. Mrs. Burke passed away on 4 July 1997.

A Navy Wife Remembers

"The Navy must always come first," he said,
said Midshipman Burke as he looked ahead
To his wedding day on the seventh of June,
And happily thought, it can't come too soon.

God must come first, she silently said,
said Bobbie herself, as she looked ahead.
Then Navy for sure, and Arleigh comes next,
"The last shall be first," according to Text.

Never alone, of this to make sure
Things in right order help love to endure.

The train trip was great to Bremerton yard,
A summer ship's overhaul didn't come hard.
The great new adventure was never uncharted,
The trail was well marked by those just departed.

The old Boston Cook-Book, the very first gift,
Philosophically taken avoided a rift.
The gravy was thin on a fresh Ensign's pay,
But "good things are free," as the song used to say.

And ideas flowed free with experienced wives,
From how to wash socks to the merits of chives.

But one summer lesson was never forgot:
When packing-time comes a husband is not.
It is then that the "Navy comes first," as he said.
Though he's apt to be last in the new home ahead.

"Travel light" is the dictum of years spent at sea,
A foot-locker household, and one trunk for me.
Imagine the impact, on orders ashore,
When thirteen big sea chests arrived at the door:

At last Ensign Arleigh came first, as I said,
Once more we joined forces for full speed ahead.

The lessons keep counting, but mainly, let's say
"When crying seems likely, just laugh it away,"
Sensibility, yes, but too sensitive, no.
Some days and sometimes when morale may be low
Make sure you are friends, for the same Golden Rule
Is the first and last of that old Navy School.

Roberta Burke

Glossary

Like any other culture, the navy has a language all its own. In navigating through life as a navy spouse, familiarity with the terminology will be very handy. Most of these terms you will pick up on your own, simply by talking with your spouse, reading navy-oriented publications, and being in the environment; inevitably, though, a few terms will come your way that send you searching for this brief glossary. I have tried to include only very common expressions (as opposed to older, historical ones) that are used in day-to-day conversation around the fleet.

1MC: The loudspeaker system on the ship that passes the word (makes announcements of general interest). On better ships, there is not a great deal of such announcing, because the *word* is put out effectively through the *chain of command* in the *plan of the day.*

Absent without leave: How a sailor's situation is described when he or she does not show up for whatever is required; normally a serious violation of navy regulations and the Uniform Code of Military Justice, leading to disciplinary action; often referred to as AWOL.

Accommodation ladder: The stairs that go up the side of the ship from the pier, barge, or small floating dock alongside the ship; often simply "ACOM ladder." These can be tricky to maneuver on, so be careful and dress comfortably when coming to the ship.

Adrift: Something that is not in its proper place; frequently used aboard ship to describe items that are left out and about the spaces on the ship. You may hear your spouse use this term in reference to household items, and may even find yourself using it to describe your teenager's room.

Airdale: Nickname for those in naval aviation (pilots, naval flight officers, air crew, etc.).

All hands: Everybody assigned to a command.

Allotment: Assignment of a portion of pay, sent automatically to a bank, address, account, or some other location; set up by the disbursing office on the ship.

Alongside: Next to or side-by-side with something else; normally associated with the movement of ships, as in "The *Barry* came alongside the *George Washington.*"

Amidships: At the center; normally associated with the ship.

ASAP: As soon as possible.

Astern: Behind the stern, or back end, of the ship.

ASW: Antisubmarine warfare.

Aye, aye: A particularly naval expression meaning, "Yes, I will comply with the order I just received."

BAQ: Basic allowance for quarters.

BAS: Basic allowance for subsistence.

Batten down: To prepare for a storm, as in "batten down the hatches"; any preparation for a struggle.

Battle E: Award given to an exceptionally capable ship, submarine, or aircraft squadron; highly prized.

Bear a hand: To hurry up and lend a hand to a common effort.

Bell; ship's bell: Found at all commands (including shore stations and squadrons); rung for ceremonial events. If your child is born while you are assigned to a command, you can ask to have the baby baptized in the ship's bell. The child's name will then be inscribed in the bell.

BEQ: Bachelor allowance for quarters.

Blackshoe: Slang expression for a sailor associated with surface ships; compare to *bubble head* or *brownshoe.*

Bluejacket: Enlisted man or woman E-1 through E-6; from the jacket worn with working uniform.

Boondoggle: A business trip that turns into something more closely resembling a vacation. For example, if your spouse is sent to San Diego for a temporary duty assignment (perhaps a school) in the middle of the winter from your home in Washington, D.C.—especially when you find out his or her school is letting out at 3:00 P.M. every day and the golf course is beckoning—you might describe the trip as a boondoggle.

Bow: The front end (normally the pointed end) of the ship; the direction it moves when going ahead

Bravo zulu: Well done, shipmate; also abbreviated "BZ."

Bridge: The place on the ship, normally located high and forward, from which the ship is driven.

Brow: The narrow plank that connects a ship or submarine from the pier to the deck; typically how you enter the ship, as in "crossing the brow."

Brownshoe: Slang expression for a sailor associated with aviation, either as a flier or a member of a squadron.

Bubblehead: Slang expression for a sailor associated with submarines.

Bulkhead: Wall.

Buoy: An object placed in the water around which a ship can navigate.

BuPers: The Bureau of Naval Personnel, where orders come from and personnel policies are formulated.

CACO: Casualty assistance calls officer; someone assigned to provide information to the family in the event of injury to a service member.

Captain's mast: Disciplinary proceeding at which a sailor appears before his or her CO for punishment after minor infractions; often called simply "mast"; compare with *court-martial.*

Chain of command: An expression to describe the chain of bosses that works its way up and down throughout the navy. This is the bedrock of the service, and it is important that all active-duty members respect it; navy spouses, on the other hand, are not part of the chain of command.

CHAMPUS: An insurance option that is part of the navy's medical system.

Chief of Naval Operations: The leader of the navy; a four-star admiral; commonly referred to as CNO.

Chief of the boat: Or COB; the command master chief of a submarine; a traditional term.

Chief petty officer: Occupies a position between the bluejackets and officers, and comes in three ranks: chief petty officer (E-7), senior chief petty officer (E-8), and master chief petty officer (E-9); self-described "backbone" of the navy.

ChInfo: Chief of naval information, the navy's leading public affairs officer; used generically for those associated with media relations.

Chit: A form to request a privilege, such as time off or earned leave on certain dates.

Chow: Food served on the ship; a "chow line" is the line of sailors awaiting chow; related to "feeder," as in "My ship has great chow; she's a real feeder."

CinC: Commander in chief, as in CinCPac (Commander in Chief, Pacific), CinCUSNavEur (Commander in Chief, U.S. Naval Forces Europe), for example.

Colors: Twice-daily ceremony (8:00 A.M. and sunset) when the American flag (at the *fantail*) and the navy *ensign* are *hauled up* and *hauled down.* If you are walking on a ship or base during colors, you will know when this occurs because the sailors will stop what they are doing and face the nearest flag at attention. Do the same.

Command duty officer: The individual in charge of the ship, on behalf of the captain and *executive officer,* while in port; often referred to as CDO. After working hours, this officer is charged with the overall safety, security, and routine of the command. The entire duty section reports to the CDO.

Command financial specialist: A member of a command with training in managing finances and preparing tax returns; can be accessed through the *ombudsman* or *command master chief.*

Commanding officer: commonly referred to as CO.

Command master chief: The E-9 assigned to a command charged with reporting directly to the CO on all aspects of enlisted relations within the command; has a particular focus on morale; often simply "master chief"; frequently works extensively with the *ombudsman.*

Court-martial: A military court for serious offenses. The difference between this and the *captain's mast:* a court-martial imposes penalties up to life imprisonment, or the death penalty, whereas a captain's mast imposes only restriction to the ship for up to sixty days, loss of pay up to a half month or two months, extra duties for up to forty-five days, or (very rare) bread and water for up to three days. Hopefully your spouse won't have any firsthand experience of all that.

DDS: Direct deposit system, which sends pay directly to a checking account.

Deck: Floor (or whatever you happen to be standing on).

Dependent's cruise: A day cruise wherein dependents are invited to come to sea and witness what sailors do for a living.

Deploy: When a seagoing command departs (the United States) and moves forward for a defined period, generally 180 days.

Detailer: The individual working at *BuPers* who discusses choices for duty, negotiates orders, and physically writes the orders that move families.

Disbursing office: The office at the command where pay records are kept, money is provided to pay bills and salaries, and checks can be cashed.

DoD: Department of Defense.

Duty: The officers and crew who must remain aboard the ship overnight while the ship is in port; normally about one-fourth to one-fifth of the crew, meaning a sailor will spend about one night in four or five away from home, even when the ship is in port. This used to be routinely about one night in three; the navy is working to make it even less.

EAOS: End of active obligated service; the end of an enlisted person's "hitch" or the end of an officer's obligated service.

Ensign: A small, special flag at the *bow.*

ETA, ETR: Estimated time of arrival, estimated time of return. When referring to a ship, one must clarify from the source exactly where the ETA/ETR is set for—e.g., pier side, the sea buoy, buoy 1A—then get a translation for pier side, which is what the navy spouse will need.

Eval: Evaluation; the annual "report card" on a sailor's performance (E-1 through E-9); compare with *fitrep.*

Executive officer: The second in command of the ship; commonly referred to as XO. Sometimes used with various adjectives (not always pleasant ones) appearing before XO. He or she is in charge of the day-to-day operation of the ship, reporting directly to the captain. This is a demanding job, held down by a very busy person on most ships.

Fantail: Large after deck on a ship.

Fast cruise: A day (or two) spent tied up to the pier but pretending to be under way; occasionally made quite realistic, with watches changing and drills conducted, usually including *general quarters.* The purpose is to practice going to sea, and ships conduct one after being in port for thirty days or more.

Field day: A cleaning project. On the ship, normally a morning or afternoon devoted to cleaning the ship; can also be applied to a single item, as in "field day the garage."

Fitrep: Fitness report; an officer's evaluation.

Flag or *flag officer:* An admiral; referring to the fact that an admiral can have a flag flown on the ship he is embarked in (aboard). One may hear, "The flag says we have to do a better job at pier security," for example.

Flank speed: Going very fast; about as fast as the ship will go.

Forecastle: The very forward part of the ship, where the people from First Division do most of the work (pronounced "folk-sul").

FPO: Fleet post office; where mail to sailors is addressed.

FSA: Family separation allowance.

Gear: A sailor's belongings, as in "Get your gear and come down here." Gear is normally kept in a locker onboard the ship.

General quarters: The process in which everyone must move quickly and smoothly to preassigned stations throughout the ship when the ship is preparing to go into battle or is responding to damage, fire, or flooding.

Hash mark: The stripes on the sleeve of an enlisted uniform signifying the amount of time the individual has in the service; four years for every stripe. They "turn to gold" if one has perfect conduct (i.e., no captain's masts) after receiving two of the hash marks.

Haul down: To lower (as a flag).

Haul up: To raise (as a flag).

Head: Bathroom.

Hull: The main body of the ship.

HUMS: Humanitarian discharge or reassignment; granted when a service member has a grave family situation (e.g., a dying child or spouse), although a discharge before a sailor's "hitch" is over is far more common than reassignment closer to home and off sea duty.

JAG: Judge Advocate General; the navy's corps of lawyers.

Knot: Nautical miles per hour; the speed of the ship.

LDO: Limited duty officer. An enlisted individual who obtains a commission is either an LDO or a warrant officer. Both are highly respected for their knowledge and experience. Also called "mustangs"; the process is often referred to as "coming up through the ranks."

LES: Leave and earning statement; a summary received each month showing how much pay a sailor has received, how much is withheld (taxes, charitable contributions, social security, advance pay), and how much leave has been accumulated and spent in the year.

Liberty: Time off. Starts with liberty call, which once was a trumpet call (tune). Also used to describe special time off, as in "I asked for special liberty"; see *liberty party.*

Liberty party: The sailors permitted ashore after working hours.

Master chief petty officer of the navy: Or MCPON (pronounced "mickpon"); a unique position in the navy for an E-10; wears a third star over his or her "crow" (as opposed to the two stars of a master chief), and advises the CNO in much the same manner as a command master chief advises the CO of an individual unit. The MCPON's office is in Washington, D.C., and includes a staff.

Mess bill: A monthly payment made by an officer to cover the costs of meals; does not apply to enlisted personnel.

Mess deck: Where the crew eats; considered the center of social life and dining on a ship, and is a gathering place during off duty time to watch movies, play cards, and socialize.

Missing ship's movement: To miss the departure of the command to sea; very serious offense.

Motor whale boat: A ship's boat, used to transport people and parts back and forth from the pier to the ship when the ship is at anchor.

MWR: Morale, welfare, and recreation; the office on the base or ship that administers "fun" programs for the command.

NAB, NAS, NAVSTA: Three different kinds of bases: naval amphibious base, naval station, naval aviation station.

NROTC: Naval Reserve Officer Training Corps; a program that provides college scholarships for individuals who then undertake a commitment to become officers (up to an eight-year active-duty obligation). The NROTC, U.S. Naval Academy, and Officer Candidate School are the most common ways of obtaining a commission in the navy.

Nuke: An individual trained in nuclear engineering and therefore assigned to ships propelled by nuclear power (all submarines and nearly all aircraft carriers are nuclear powered; there are very few remaining nuclear surface ships). Nukes draw extra pay in recognition of their extra schooling.

OCS: Officer Candidate School; located in Newport, Rhode Island, where an individual with a college degree can attend and obtain a commission in the U.S. Navy.

Officer of the deck; junior officer of the deck: In port, the individuals who keep watch on the quarterdeck of the ship, ensuring the security, safety, and execution of the ship's routine; at sea, the officers on the bridge who keep watch and navigate the ship. Often referred to as OOD or JOOD, they report to the CDO.

Old Man: Older slang term for the CO; obviously losing currency as more females ascend to command navy ships and squadrons. A more common slang term is "skipper."

Ombudsman: Person appointed by the CO to help maintain communication between the command and the crew's families.

OPNAV: The staff of the CNO in Washington, D.C.

OPPE/ORSE: Two engineering inspections, the ORSE for nuclear-powered ships and the OPPE for all other ships; pronounced "op-pee" and "ors." A sailor will face hard work and be very busy for six months before inspections if he or she is an engineer.

Overhead: Ceiling (or whatever is above your head).

PCS: Permanent change of station.

Plan of the day: A small daily one- to two-page newsletter distributed every evening at a command describing the next day's events and informing of upcoming events, command philosophy, awards, and other bits of information; commonly referred to as P-O-D. Some commands encourage sailors to take these home for the family to read.

Port: To the left.

Postal clerk: Ship's mailperson.

PSD: Personnel support detachment.

Public affairs officer: A navy officer specializing in media relations.

Quarterdeck: The entryway to the ship, submarine, or squadron space; the ceremonial heart of the command, where the officer of the deck in port, petty officer of the watch, and messenger of the watch stand duty.

Quarters: A morning formation or muster (where everyone lines up and stands at attention to see who is present); general announcements are usually made at quarters: the *word* is put out by the *chain of command*, such as "The captain wants us to do a better job of helping new people when they get aboard; here's the plan."

Rack: A bed; correct term on the ship is "bunk," but rack is universally used, as in "hitting the rack" (going to bed).

Sail: To get under way. Obviously navy ships no longer actually sail, but the term is still common, as in "We sail at 0600."

SecDef: Secretary of defense.

SecNav: Secretary of the navy.

SGLI: Serviceman's Group Life Insurance.

Shakedown: Getting the ship or submarine under way after some time in the yards (undergoing repairs) or a long time by the pier; also something new ships do after they are built to ensure they are ready to be turned over to the navy.

Shore patrol: Sailors ashore who act as liaisons to the police and provide discipline to the *liberty party* on the beach.

Skipper: The CO; most often used by aviators.

Smoking lamp: An expression indicating whether or not smoking is permitted on the ship, as in "The smoking lamp is lit [you can smoke] in the chief's mess." In general, there are fewer places and times when smoking is permitted on navy ships these days, so plan on not being able to smoke on the ship.

Snipe: An individual who works in the engineering department.

Squared away: Something (a piece of equipment or a process) that is in good working order; a space that is neatly stowed; a person who is very efficient and professional; as in "The check-in procedure on the USS *Barry* for new people is squared away" or "The gun mount is squared away" or "Chief Jones is squared away."

Starboard: To the right.

Stern: Back end of the ship, where the *fantail* is located.

Superstructure: The part of the ship above the main deck.

Swab: A mop onboard the ship (the old-fashioned kind with strings).

TAD, TDY: Used interchangeably, meaning temporary duty area from normal duty station, as in "My husband is TAD in Omaha for two weeks."

Tiger cruise: A chance for a few guests to ride the ship for several days; generally conducted at the end of a six-month deployment, with dependents and friends flying to meet the ship in some overseas port (e.g., Hawaii on the West Coast and Bermuda on the East Coast) and riding the ship the remaining three to five days of the deployment. A wonderful experience, and recently opened up to female as well as male dependents on most ships.

Topside: The upper decks of the ship.

UA: Unauthorized absence.

UCMJ: Uniform Code of Military Justice; the laws of the military.

VHA: Variable housing allowance; the extra pay a sailor receives to cover the cost of living in high-cost areas. The total money given for housing is VHA plus *BAQ.*

Wake: The churning water behind a ship as it passes through the sea.

Watch: A period of duty at an assigned station on a ship.

Word: Information concerning an upcoming event or set of rules, as in "Seaman Smith didn't get the word about the ship getting under way early, so she missed movement." The word is passed out via the *plan of the day,* at *quarters,* over the *1MC,* or by the *chain of command.*

Yards: The repair shop for ships and submarines; generally a dirty, noisy, and unpleasant place for a sailor to work. On the other hand, he or she will be home every night (except for duty nights) because sailors won't go out to sea while in the yard.

If you think you already know navy lingo, try translating this letter. If you know everything in it, you pass; if not, keep studying the glossary.

Dear Mary,

Life is busy here aboard the USS *Always Gone.* The airdales are here, so chow lines are longer than ever on the mess deck. I've been standing watch on the quarterdeck while we're in port. I'll be able to go on liberty tomorrow.

The weather was so rough during this past underway period that we were walking on the bulkheads. I hope it calms down soon.

Jonesy went UA from the last port and the skipper is really mad. If he shows up here, he'll go right to mast.

I'm glad you have the DDS problem straightened out and that our BAQ and VHA have finally kicked in. We'll start FSA really soon too.

I'll talk to my detailer next week and start to plan our PCS move. Shore duty looks good to me right now.

Well, gotta go. The master chief is yelling for all hands to field day. I can't wait to hit the rack.

Love, Mike

Resources

Organizations and Programs for Navy Spouses and Families

American Red Cross: National headquarters located at 17th and D Streets NW, Washington, D.C., 20006; telephone 202-737-8300. Red Cross local offices are listed in the telephone directory.

Armed Forces Hostess Association: These volunteers are a group of military spouses who will provide information on military bases all over the world to families transferring to new duty stations. Their central location is in the Pentagon, Room 1A736, Washington, D.C. 20310-3133.

Chaplain's Program: Navy chaplains are fully trained and ordained priests, ministers, or rabbis who minister to military personnel and their families. They are assets to any command. The local base directory, NFSC, or command ombudsman will provide the telephone numbers and direct interested people to the chaplains' offices. In Washington, D.C., the Chief of Navy Chaplains office can be reached at 703-614-4043.

Dental Plan, TRICARE for active-duty family members: The program under United Concordia that provides dental care. A dental benefits booklet is available at FMDP Customer Service, P.O. Box 898218, Camp Hill, PA 17089-8218; telephone 1-800-866-8499.

Exceptional Family Member Program: The navy program designed to identify family members with long-term health care or special educational needs. The local NFSC can provide details on the program, or call 1-800-527-8830.

Family Advocacy Program: A command and family advocacy program partnership committed to the prevention of child and spouse abuse in the navy community. Contact the local NFSC or the headquarters organization at the Naval Station, Bldg. 150, 2701 South Capitol Street SW, Washington, D.C. 20373; telephone 202-433-5032.

Morale, Welfare, and Recreation (MWR): Exist at every level in the navy and are found at virtually every base and organization. The office manages a range of programs focused on quality-of-life issues—child care, social clubs, restaurants, parks, trips, and so forth. They are supported from profits generated from the navy exchange system and user fees. To locate, check with the command ombudsman or command master chief, or use the base directory.

National Military Family Association (NMFA): National organization dedicated to identifying and resolving issues of concern to military families. Essentially an advocate for uniformed service families in the Washington, D.C., area. Located at 2500 North Van Dorn Street, Suite 102, Alexandria, VA 22302-1601; telephone 703-823-6632.

Naval Services FamilyLine: An all-volunteer, nonprofit, tax-exempt organization dedicated to improving the quality of life for sea service families. They publish materials on all aspects of navy life. These materials are available by writing or telephoning their main office at 1254 9th Street SE, Suite 104, Washington Navy Yard, Washington, D.C. 20374; telephone 202-433-2333, e-mail <nsfamline@aol.com>, or through the NFSC. A sampling of their current set of publications:

Financial and Personal Affairs
Guidelines for the Spouses of Command Master Chiefs and Chiefs of the Boat
Guidelines for the Spouses of Commanding and Executive Officers
Launching Clubs or Support Groups for Navy and Marine Corps Spouses
Ombudsman Journal
Overseasmanship (a booklet to help prepare spouses and families for a tour of duty overseas)
Sea Legs for the Navy Family (a compact handbook to assist with transition into the navy)
Social Customs and Traditions of the Sea Services
Welcome Aboard (a brochure for new spouses)

Navy Family Service Center: Their programs and materials cover relocation, employment, life skills, education, support, counseling, volunteer programs, crisis response, mobilization and deployment support, personal finances, tax assistance, transition assistance, family advocacy, exceptional family members, and many other subjects. Check the local base directory for the closest center or call 1-800-FSC-LINE.

Navy League of the United States: A large and influential organization that promotes the interests of the sea services. They publish a magazine of defense and maritime affairs called *Sea Power*. Their address is Navy League of the United States, 2300 Wilson Blvd., Arlington, VA 22201; telephone 1-800-356-5760.

Navy Legal Service Office: Located on all major bases. The navy's JAG corps provides free legal advice and assistance regarding your personal and professional legal needs in a variety of situations. Understand, however, that certain personal matters are beyond their charter; one would need to hire a private attorney, for example, in the case of personal lawsuits. Check with NLSO before engaging private counsel. Their number is in the base directory.

Navy–Marine Corps Relief Society: A nonprofit charitable organization that assists navy and Marine Corps personnel and their families in times of need. The headquarters is at 801 North Randolph Street, Suite 1228, Arlington, VA 22203-1978; telephone 703-696-4904. Local chapters are located in every center of fleet concentration, but the national headquarters can refer you to helpful resources or provide information.

Navy Mutual Aid Association: Offers low-cost insurance to active-duty navy, Marine Corps, and Coast Guard personnel. Their headquarters address is Arlighton Annex, Room G-9070, Washington, D.C. 20370-0001; telephone 1-800-628-6011.

Navy Wives Clubs of America: The country's only national federation of navy spouses. It consists of thirteen navy-oriented volunteer organizations. They have pamphlets, ideas, and other information available. The address is Navy Wives Clubs of America, P.O. Box 2606, Jacksonville, FL 32203-2606.

Non-Commissioned Officers Association: A federally chartered organization that promotes and protects the rights and benefits of noncommissioned officers and veterans of all branches of the armed forces. Their address is NCOA, 10635 IH 35 N, San Antonio, TX 78265; telephone 1-800-662-2620.

Ombudsman Program: Ensures that each command has a trained individual able to provide better communication between navy families and the chain of command. Nationally, the address is Ombudsman Program, Department of the Navy (BuPers 66), Washington, D.C. 20370-5066; telephone 703-697-6550.

Overseas Schools Information: The overseas schools organization is located at Department of Defense Dependent Schools, Hoffman Building I, Room 152, 2461 Eisenhower Ave., Alexandria, VA 22331.

Overseas Transfer Information Service: Provides basic information on moving overseas through the sponsor program. The telephone number is 1-800-327-8197.

The Retired Officers Association (TROA): An independent, nonprofit service organization that represents uniformed personnel on Capitol Hill and provides retirement information, advice and assistance, post-retirement job placement, and other services. They publish a magazine, *The Retired Officer.* Their address is TROA, 201 N. Washington Street, Alexandria, VA 22314-2529; telephone 1-800-245-TROA.

Spouse Employment Assistance Program: Helps navy spouses find employment in new areas. The program is administered locally by the NFSC.

United Services Organization (USO): Provides educational, self-help, and recreational programs to military members and their families worldwide. The world headquarters is located at 1008 Eberle Place, SE, Suite 301, Washington, D.C. 20374-5096, telephone 1-800-876-7469.

Books, Guides, Pamphlets, Periodicals

It is a good idea to build up a basic "library" of guides and pamphlets by visiting the NFSC and base library, where most sources are available.

Keep the sources in a box in the garage, or in a file folder in the closet. You will find that many of your questions can be answered by referring to this free "navy library."

All Hands: Magazine published monthly by the navy that includes a wide variety of information for the navy spouse. It is available through the command or at the NFSC, base library, or chaplain's office. Try to obtain a copy of the annual "owner's and operator's" issue, which covers a great deal of useful information for sailors and their spouses.

Fisher House Magazine: Published quarterly, this journal discusses the option of staying at a low-cost Fisher House while a child is sick in a navy hospital. Information is available from the Intrepid Museum, Intrepid Square, West 46th St. and 12th Ave., New York, NY 10036; telephone 212-245-2533. Further information on staying at a Fisher House is also available at the NFSC or the navy hospital itself.

"Guide to U.S. Military Installations": An annual special supplement to the *Navy Times,* this pamphlet includes detailed information on over 250 major bases, posts, and stations all around the country. It covers housing, health, commissaries, exchanges, base closings, and Internet e-mail addresses.

"Handbook for Military Families": An annual supplement to the spring issue of the *Navy Times*. Be sure to buy this issue and keep the handbook. It is filled with useful information on every aspect of military family life.

Marriage and Military Life: A useful pamphlet designed to help couples evaluate the strengths and weaknesses of their relationship. Available from the NFSC or the base chaplain's center.

"Married to the Military": An annual supplement to the spring issue of the *Navy Times*. A handy pamphlet worth keeping in your library.

Naval Ceremonies, Customs, and Traditions (Vice Adm. William P. Mack, USN [Ret] and Lt. Cdr. Royal W. Connell, USN. Naval Institute Press, 1987): Provides a broad look at the uniformed side of the navy.

Naval station newspapers: Every base will have one or two newspapers that are distributed free. Copies can be picked up at the navy exchange or commissary. Larger bases have particularly large weekly papers, such as the *Flagship* published in the Norfolk area. These newspapers are useful as sources of information and as a way to publicize events for a support group or command. Most, for example, will run announcements of meeting times and locations or stories about navy families.

Navy Family Lifeline: An authorized quarterly publication produced by the navy (through the Naval Media Center) and available through the command. Copies also available at the NFSC or from the Naval Media Center, Naval Station Anacostia, Washington, D.C. 20374.

Navy Times: An excellent, albeit expensive, weekly newspaper and a good resource for navy spouses, this publication provides in-depth coverage of virtually every issue of importance to navy spouses. Sailors will enjoy it as well. If the cost is over a family's budget, it is available at the base library, but be sure to buy at least the issues that include the following excellent annual supplements for permanent reference: "Handbook for Military Families," "Guide to U.S. Military Installations," "Married to the Military," and "CHAMPUS." To subscribe, call 1-800-368-5418.

On Watch: Periodical published by the Fleet Reserve Association in the interests of active-duty (regular and reserve) U.S. Navy, Marine Corps, and Coast Guard personnel. Write to Fleet Reserve Association, 125 North West Street, Alexandria, VA 22314-2752; telephone 1-800-FRA-1924.

Proceedings: A monthly professional journal of the U.S. Navy, published by the U.S. Naval Institute. Articles cover a wide range of naval issues, including many of interest to spouses. A subscription is best obtained by joining the U.S. Naval Institute. Call 1-800-233-8764.

Relocation Ready Reference Handbook: Available at the NFSC or the base library, this publication provides information and guidance for moves from one installation to another, as well as information for those leaving the military.

Service Etiquette (Oretha D. Swartz. Naval Institute Press, 1988): An excellent guide on manners and all aspects of naval etiquette.

TRICARE Handbook: Covers the entire TRICARE system and is a baseline publication for working with civilian medical care. Copies can be found at the NFSC or the closest navy hospital or medical facility. The *Navy Times* also publishes an annual TRICARE supplement in one of their spring issues. Get this issue and keep the supplement.

Uniformed Services Journal: Serving all personnel of the uniformed services, this bimonthly journal is produced to support legislation that is beneficial to the security of the United States, sustains the moraie of the armed forces, and is supportive of all members of the armed forces. Their offices are located at 5535 Hempstead Way, Springfield, VA 22151-4094; telephone 703-750-1342.

U.S. Forces Travel and Transfer Guide: An all-ranks guide to moving published by Military Living Publications, P.O. Box 2347, Falls Church, VA 22042; telephone 703-237-2233. This company also publishes *Military "Space-A" Air Opportunities* and *Military "Space-A" Air Basic Training,* both of which can help you travel free on government air, and they publish *Temporary Military Lodging—Travel on Less Per Day . . . the Military Way,* a handy book on obtaining inexpensive military lodging. These publications are usually available at the NFSC and base library, as well as directly from the company.

Finally, keep the *Navy Spouse's Guide* handy, and be sure to look into the many other books and publications of interest to the navy spouse published by the Naval Institute Press. They also publish hundreds of titles that deal with naval history, traditions, customs, and current issues, and their books make wonderful gifts for the navy family. The Naval Institute Press catalogue can be obtained by calling 1-800-233-8764.

Index

deployments: activities for those at home, 104–8; checklists, 151–54; dealing with challenges, 147–50; finances during, 40–41

destroyers, 17–18

detailer, 22

dining in and out, 89

direct deposit, 38–39

dislocation allowance, 120

divine worship, 103–4

division officer's spouse, 167–68

division parties, 96–97

"Don't give up the ship," 14

door-to-door move, 113

e-mail, 75–76

emergency communications, 65

emergency file, 75–76

emergency leave, 64

employment for navy spouses, 59

entertaining, 93–98

Exceptional Family Member (EFM) Program, 78–80

executive officer spouse, 168–69

expiration of active obligated service (EAOS), 155

Family Advocacy Program (FAP), 60

family service centers (NFSC), 35–36, 58–61

family support group, 91–93

files: emergency, 75–76; important day-to-day, 36

finances: allotments, 39–40; basic finance, 41–43; bills, 44; direct deposit, 43; deployment concerns, 45–46; "money stealers," 43; planning, 51–53; predeployment issues, 159

financial planning, "5–10–20 year plan," 46

Fisher Houses at navy hospitals, 51

fleet, 16–19

frigates, 20

growing up in the navy, 2

history of the navy, 12–15

holiday ideas during deployments, 107–8

holiday party, 88

hospitality kits from Navy Family Service Centers, 35

household goods, 111

house hunting, 122

hurricanes, 73–75

identification cards, obtaining, 36–37

insurance, 44–45

kids in the navy, 2, 5–7

King, Ernest, 14

language overseas, 134–35

Leahy, William, 14

leave and earning statement (LES), 29

legal assistance, 51–52; Judge Advocate General (JAG, navy lawyer), 52; Navy Legal Service Office, 38; potential legal issues, 51–52; predeployment issues, 52–53

life in the navy, 1–2

LIFElines, 54–55

MAC flights. *See* military flights

media relations, 73

medical: advanced care, 47–49; basic care, 31–32; DEERS, 31; TRICARE, 47–49; TRICARE costs, 49

military affiliated radio system (MARS), 71

military courtesy, 102–3

military flights, 136–37

mobile homes, 118

moving: checklists, 114–16, 122–25; claims, 119–20; crating household goods, 112–13; do-it-yourself (DITY), 118–19; frequent moves, 167; movers, 112–16; moving day, 128; Personal Property Shipping (or Transportation) Office, 111, 112–13; philosophy, 110–12; relocation assistance, 59; setting it up, 111–12; unpacking at destination, 115–16; weight limits, 126

Naval Personnel, Bureau of. *See* BuPers

NAVCARE clinic, 33

navy birthday, 12; Navy Birthday Ball, 90

About the Author

A native of Jacksonville, Florida, and the daughter of a naval aviator, Laura Hall Stavridis grew up in the navy and has lived on naval bases all over the world. She graduated from Rogers High School in Newport, Rhode Island, while her father served at the Naval War College.

After graduating in 1981 from Dickinson College with majors in political science and French, she married a surface line officer in the U.S. Naval Academy chapel. She and her husband have moved ten times in fifteen years, and have lived in navy homeports on both coasts. Her husband completed over two years in command of a guided missile destroyer and is currently assigned to the Joint Staff in the Pentagon.

Mrs. Stavridis was awarded an M.A. in international relations from Boston University, where she also taught political science and conducted doctoral work. She was the recipient of several university fellowships during her two years there.

In the Washington area, she has worked at the World Bank and participated in volunteer work with the Literacy Council of Northern Virginia. Mrs. Stavridis now resides in Mount Vernon with her husband, Jim, and two daughters, Christina and Julia.

The Naval Institute Press is the book-publishing arm of the U.S. Naval Institute, a private, nonprofit, membership society for sea service professionals and others who share an interest in naval and maritime affairs. Established in 1873 at the U.S. Naval Academy in Annapolis, Maryland, where its offices remain today, the Naval Institute has members worldwide.

Members of the Naval Institute support the education programs of the society and receive the influential monthly magazine *Proceedings* and discounts on fine nautical prints and on ship and aircraft photos. They also have access to the transcripts of the Institute's Oral History Program and get discounted admission to any of the Institute-sponsored seminars offered around the country. Discounts are also available to the colorful bimonthly magazine *Naval History*.

The Naval Institute's book-publishing program, begun in 1898 with basic guides to naval practices, has broadened its scope to include books of more general interest. Now the Naval Institute Press publishes about one hundred titles each year, ranging from how-to books on boating and navigation to battle histories, biographies, ship and aircraft guides, and novels. Institute members receive significant discounts on the Press's more than eight hundred books in print.

Full-time students are eligible for special half-price membership rates. Life memberships are also available.

For a free catalog describing Naval Institute Press books currently available, and for further information about joining the U.S. Naval Institute, please write to:

Membership Department
U.S. Naval Institute
291 Wood Road
Annapolis, MD 21402-5034
Telephone: (800) 233-8764
Fax: (410) 269-7940
Web address: www.navalinstitute.org